12th GRADE READY

EXPERT ADVICE TO HELP PARENTS NAVIGATE THE YEAR AHEAD

EDITED BY
TIMOTHY M. DOVE

A READY GUIDE

PARENT **READY**.

PARENT READY.

2024 Edition
Copyright © 2024 Parent Ready, Inc.

Parent Ready supports the right to free expression and the value of copyright. The purpose of copyright is to encourage the creation of works that enrich our culture.

All rights reserved. No part of this book may be reprinted or reproduced in any form or by any electronic, mechanical, or other means, now known or hereafter invented, including photocopying, recording, and information storage and retrieval, without the prior written permission of the publisher, except in the case of brief quotations embodied in critical articles and reviews.

Published by Parent Ready, Inc.
8 East Windsor Avenue
Alexandria, Virginia 22301
https://parentready.com

Parent Ready and design are trademarks of Parent Ready, Inc.

The publisher is not responsible for websites (or their contents) that are not owned by the publisher.

ISBN: 979-8-9893392-4-2 (paperback)
ISBN: 979-8-9893392-3-5 (e-book)

Bulk purchases: Quantity discounts are available. Please make inquiries via https://gradeready.guide.

Table of Contents

Contributors vii
Foreword xiii
   Andrea Sachs
Introduction xvii
   Timothy M. Dove

Chapter 1: How Is 12th Grade Different from 11th Grade? 1
   Celebrating the milestones while preparing for the next step
   Lorynn Guerrero

Chapter 2: How Is a 12th Grader Different from an
   11th Grader? 9
   Notes on the triangular nature of education—parents,
      students, and teachers
   Darryl Johnson

Chapter 3: Choosing Classes 19
   How to understand your student's course selections
   Mary Lou Mendoza

Chapter 4: Inclusion 29
   How to support your student's identity, safety, and allyship
   Shari Collins

Chapter 5: Building Study Skills 37
   How to support your student in taking ownership
      of their learning
   Al Rabanera

Chapter 6: Overcoming Academic Setbacks 47
    How to help your 12th grader with resilience, self-reflection, and independence
    Antoine Sharpe

Chapter 7: Overcoming Procrastination 61
    How to support your student in finding motivation
    Leron McAdoo

Chapter 8: Navigating Student-Teacher Relationships 71
    How to help your senior build rapport with educators
    Amybeth Taylor

Chapter 9: Planning the Postsecondary Route 83
    How your student's high school helps with the process
    Courtney Walker

Chapter 10: Online Presence 95
    How to help your student own their online narrative
    Timothy M. Dove

Chapter 11: The Senior Slump. 107
    How to identify and support your high schooler through senioritis
    Casie Wise, EdD

Chapter 12: Finding What You Love to Do…In and Out of School 119
    How the search for passions extends past high school
    Laura Jeanne Penrod

Chapter 13: Congratulations, You Have a Senior! 127
    How will I know if my teen is ready for what's next?
    Jessica Volker

This series of books is dedicated to all those who contribute to the education and support of young people. I was lucky enough to be a classroom teacher for 32 years. I owe a lot of my effectiveness to those who worked with me and those who taught me so much over the years, especially two master educators, Jenelle and Mark Dove, my parents. Our parents and classroom teachers encourage, question, teach, and celebrate our students. I want to thank my colleagues who participated in this project. We can always learn from one another, and having many voices in this conversation is so helpful. Thank you to all the educators who are still engaged in this sacred trust.

—*Timothy M. Dove*

Contributors

Editor

Timothy M. Dove, an educator for 42 years, is the Ohio State Teacher of the Year in 2011 and 2012. Dove was a middle school teacher for 32 years and helped develop the Global Scholars Diploma program. He taught high schoolers for three years, was an adjunct professor at The Ohio State University for 20 years, and for the past decade has worked with state and national education agencies supporting educators and students in a variety of ways. He has been a consultant with Battelle for Kids in Hong Kong, Learning Forward, the Council of Chief State School Officers (CCSSO), and the Collaboration for Effective Educator Development, Accountability, and Reform (CEEDAR) Center.

Contributors

Shari Collins, a lifelong educator in Nebraska and Iowa, specializes in training, leadership development, and Diversity, Equity, and Inclusion. With more than 25 years in the DEI field, Collins enjoys speaking, consulting, and training across the globe in various industries. In her most prized contract with the National Education Association, Collins interacts with educators across the country to promote more inclusive behaviors and positive schools for all. Collins graduated from Hastings College with a bachelor of arts and from the

University of Nebraska Omaha with a master of science. She loves reading and learning, caring for her plants, traveling, and spending time with her family, which includes two rescue Yorkie sisters.

Lorynn Guerrero is an assistant principal at Gadsden High School in Anthony, New Mexico. She taught English language arts to grades 9–12 for 16 years before transitioning into the administrative role. She is the 2022 New Mexico Teacher of the Year and a New Mexico Teach Plus Policy Fellow for the 2022–23 year. She previously taught teen parents in a GRADS (graduation, reality, and dual-role skills) program that supported them in earning their high school diplomas. She began her teaching career in Hatch, New Mexico, teaching 6th-grade English and received her first nomination for Teacher of the Year in 2008. Guerrero has a master of education with an emphasis in education administration, a bachelor of science in secondary education with an emphasis in English language arts, Advanced Placement certification in literature and composition, and Teaching English to Speakers of Other Languages (TESOL) certification.

Darryl Johnson earned his BS and MS in English education from Northwest Missouri State University, achieved National Board for Professional Teaching Standards Certification, and received Northwest Missouri State University's Young Alumni Award and the Missouri National Education Association Horace Mann Award. He has written numerous articles for regional and national journals and has given keynotes to local, regional, and national audiences. In 2007, he was named Missouri Teacher of the Year and in 2013 was inducted into the National Teachers Hall of Fame. Johnson retired from North Kansas City School District in 2021 and works for FiredUP Consulting Group.

Leron Charles McAdoo (aka Ron Mc The HipHoptimist) is a distinguished educator, artist, musician, and author. He is the first-ever poet laureate of Little Rock, Arkansas, a youth advocate, the cofounder of Backyard Enterprises, and the visionary behind The Mctivated Educational Motivation Brand. As a teacher since 1994, McAdoo has been recognized by the Arkansas Declaration of Learning, NAACP, City of Little Rock, LRSD, University of Pine Bluff, and others. McAdoo has empowered educators and students, delivered multiple TED Talks, spoken internationally, and been an Arkansas bestselling author. McAdoo aims to serve and lives to make his family proud.

Mary Lou Mendoza is the lead counselor at Gadsden High School, located in Anthony, New Mexico. She has a bachelor's degree in human services and a master's degree in professional counseling from Grand Canyon University. Mendoza grew up in Anthony and graduated from Gadsden High School in 1992. As an alumna, she is very passionate and determined to help make a difference for the students she works with. Mendoza is the mother of four amazing children and lives with her husband in El Paso, Texas.

Laura Jeanne ("Jeannie") Penrod, the 2024 Nevada State Teacher of the Year, has been a high school educator in the Clark County School District for almost 18 years. Penrod teaches disciplines ranging from special education to English language learners and varying levels of English language arts. She facilitates meaningful learning experiences with students using project-based and social-emotional learning to foster student reflection and advocacy. Penrod has engaged in local, statewide, national, and global fellowships and is passionate about teacher and student leadership. She is a contributing columnist on education for *The Nevada Independent*.

Al Rabanera, EdD, is a high school math teacher at La Vista High School in Fullerton, California. He assisted in the development and implementation of new programs that promote the retention of current teachers and encourage students to pursue careers in teaching. Rabanera is an advocate for educators. He serves on the board of directors for the Council for the Accreditation of Educator Preparation and has previously served on the boards for North Orange County United Teachers and the California Teachers Association Institute for Teaching. Rabanera was one of five educators who received the Horace Mann Award for Teaching Excellence in 2017 and was an NEA Foundation Global Learning Fellow. In 2018, he received Distinguished Alumni of the Year for the College of Education at California State University Fullerton. In 2019–20, he served as a Teach Plus California Policy Fellow and is currently a Senior National Policy Advisory Board member. Rabanera earned his doctorate from the University of Southern California. He is married to Cassandra and they have a son, Nehemiah, and a daughter, Aurora.

Andrea Sachs has been a faculty member at St. Paul Academy and Summit School since 2000. She has taught history courses throughout her tenure, and from 2013 to 2019 she also worked as a college counselor. In addition to the 11th-grade introductory U.S. history course, she has taught senior electives in historiography, women's history, the history of social movements, and the history of medicine. She has served on the executive board of the Organization of American Historians and the Teacher Advisory Council of the National Constitution Center.

Antoine Sharpe is a secondary math instructional system specialist for the Department of Defense Education Activity (DoDEA), with 18 years of educational experience. He is a National Board Certified Teacher and the 2020 Department of Defense Teacher of the Year. Sharpe is also a recipient of the PAEMST Award, recognizing his significant contributions to STEM education. Growing up as a military-connected child and now married to an Air Force officer, he has a strong commitment to assisting students and families in the military community. His work is driven by a blend of personal experiences and professional expertise.

Amybeth Taylor, who has more than 15 years of experience in secondary English education, teaches 11th- and 12th-grade students in Newmarket, New Hampshire. Her journey in education began as a Teach for America corps member in Los Angeles, California. Taylor holds a master's in education from the University of New Hampshire and a graduate certificate in ESOL instruction from California State University, Dominguez Hills. Her commitment to innovative education extends beyond the classroom, evident in her advocacy work with nonprofits and experience in curriculum design. Taylor strives to create authentic learning experiences for her students, nurturing a lifelong appreciation for literature and writing.

Jessica Volker has been in education for the past 13 years. For 12 of those years, she was a high school math teacher in Sioux Falls, South Dakota, where she was nominated for Teacher of the Year three times and was a finalist one year. She spent one year as the curriculum and instruction coordinator in Columbus, Nebraska, and currently teaches middle school math in Albion, Nebraska. Volker has her masters of education in curriculum and instruction and has her doctorate in educational administration. Not only is she passionate about teaching kids math, but she is also passionate about retaining and supporting young teachers. She is a city girl turned small-town resident and lives in Albion with her husband, Michael, and their two dogs, Winnie and Jersey.

Courtney Walker is the assistant principal of teaching and learning at Carrollton High School in Carrollton, Georgia. She oversees various responsibilities, including master scheduling, remedial and gifted programs, student awards and recognitions, and school improvement initiatives. She has implemented teacher-led professional development that incorporates data-driven instruction and a model of shared leadership. She supports school counselors in developing personalized academic plans tailored to student interest and ability to ensure that students graduate enrolled, enlisted, or employed and engaged as leaders in their communities. Walker was selected as the 2024 Georgia Association of Secondary School Principals Assistant Principal of the Year.

Dr. Casie Wise has more than 20 years of classroom and administrative experience. In addition to 12 years of teaching middle and high school English in the United States and abroad, she has also served as a K–12 school support director, instructional coach, core advocate for Tennessee, literacy adviser, and education consultant. Dr. Wise resides in her hometown of Memphis, Tennessee, with her husband, son, and daughter. She has a BSE in secondary English education from John Brown University in Arkansas, an MA in teaching English as a second language, and a doctorate in curriculum and instructional leadership from the University of Memphis.

Foreword

Andrea Sachs
History Teacher and Former College Counselor, Minnesota

If you have made it to senior year and your child is taking steps to imagine and plan their* life as a young adult, then congratulations. It's taken 17 or 18 years to get to this point, and I hope that you are seeing the positive effects of the care and effort you have put into parenting. Senior year can bring with it a lot of big feelings that bounce between unbridled joy and deep anxiety about the future—and that's just for the parents. High school seniors also experience a messy mix of emotions that are more easily managed when the adults around them convey confidence and optimism.

Parents sometimes feel a sense of urgency as senior year begins, as if this year marks their last opportunity to guide and advise their offspring before they send them out into the world. This urgency can easily transform into stress and conflict that can really suck the joy out of the year. My advice is to take a deep breath and play the long game. No matter how independent and self-sufficient your child is the day they graduate from high school, they will continue to evolve

---

* The pronoun they/them is used in its singular form throughout the book because it is the most practical and inclusive approach.

in remarkable, and often surprising, ways after they move out of your house and into their adult lives.

I've worked with high school seniors for more than 30 years as a classroom teacher and, for a six-year period, as a college counselor. Although a lot has changed since I began my career, the fundamental elements of this transitional phase have stayed consistent. My advice is rooted in my decades of observing students and their families and also in the humbling year I spent parenting my own senior and trying valiantly to follow my own advice.

If this foreword has a thesis statement (and, as a history teacher, I always want my essays to have a thesis statement), it's that senior year marks your transition to being a parent of an adult. With demographic trends and a bit of luck on your side, you will spend more years having an adult-to-adult relationship with your offspring than you spent raising them as a child. What do you want that relationship to look and feel like? How can you lay the groundwork for the new version of your relationship now, while you are living in the same house? How can you guide your child while recognizing their growing autonomy?

Virtually all of the parents I've worked with want to see their children enjoy their final year of high school and arrive at graduation day with great options and a solid plan. Imagining the final outcome is the easy part; much more challenging is the process of working toward that moment. They want to help their children build confidence and resilience, but the stakes can feel so high. To me, this balance—supporting independence while offering guidance—is the trickiest but most important parenting challenge. One way to find that middle ground is to think of senior year as an experiential lesson in complex decision-making. It might be the first time your child navigates through a process this complicated, but it won't be the last. What habits of mind and heart can you help them cultivate? How can you model optimism in the face of uncertainty? How can you communicate, and operate within, a clearly defined set of parameters? How can you support and guide your child without taking too much control away from them? How can you share exciting family news while honoring your child's privacy? How can you help your child finish the year on a strong note, even as they anticipate big changes ahead? Thinking through these questions early on will help you navigate the year with care and intention.

I want to end by offering the psychological concept known as "creeping determinism" as a framework that I have found immensely helpful. I first encountered this term in a 2003 *The New Yorker* article by Malcolm Gladwell titled "Connecting the Dots," where he reflected on intelligence experts' failure to anticipate, and thwart, the devastating attacks of September 11, 2001. Creeping determinism, he explained, means that, although we can usually connect the dots or trace the origins of events that have already happened, clarity and certainty fall away when we map a path toward the future.

We can look back and connect the dots in our own lives: the course we took as an undergraduate that steered us toward our major, the summer job that helped us clarify our career plans, the mentors who guided us, and many other pivotal experiences. What we sometimes forget is that nothing is inevitable; the path we took was just one of many that we could have taken. Your child is at the front end of this process, with a seemingly infinite range of possibilities before them. Guided by the lessons, skills, and habits that you have helped them internalize, they will find their way and chart their own course.

Introduction

Timothy M. Dove
2011 & 2012 Ohio State Teacher of the Year

This book is for parents, family members, caregivers, siblings, mentors, and any supporters of a soon-to-be 12th grader. Think of each of these chapters as advice from a friendly teacher in your child's school.

For those of you embarking on the experience of having a high school senior in your family for the first time, you'll find loads of information useful to you and your student.

Each contributor to *12th Grade Ready* is a current or former 12th-grade educator who has worked extensively with parents and families of students. These contributors have all been Teachers of the Year, finalists, or recognized for their abilities in their state. They are experts in the field overall and in the subjects of the chapters they penned.

The chapters that follow cover many of the topics that you may be thinking about as your teen enters 12th grade. Beginning with how 12th grade differs from 11th and moving through preparing them for life beyond 12th grade, this book will serve as your guide. It will describe what to expect in a variety of areas and things to look for as you navigate your young adult's physical, emotional, and academic growth. This book focuses on both action items and tips on how to support your student as they continue developing their independence.

Some information might seem obvious, while other pieces will be eye-opening. Every family is different, and parts of the book will resonate differently with each reader. Any new information can help you plan and engage with your high school senior. That with which you are already familiar should assure you that you are on the right track.

Most chapters give prompts throughout or conclude with a list of conversation starters. In thinking about how to use them, consider your student's history, your relationship with them, and other family dynamics. Using open-ended questions is the best way to get information from your student. Not only will having these conversations assist you in supporting your 12th grader, but they will also open new lines of communication that can continue throughout the school year. You can focus on the chapters needed, or of interest, or you can read it straight through for a survey of the year that might spark ideas.

The 12th grade is an emotional year of change for you and your teen. Everyone realizes the end of high school is on the horizon. This realization adds anxiety and excitement for the near future. We hope this book helps you navigate the journey.

Chapter 1
HOW IS 12TH GRADE DIFFERENT FROM 11TH GRADE?

Celebrating the milestones while preparing for the next step

Lorynn Guerrero
2022 New Mexico State Teacher of the Year

Big congratulations to you and your family—you officially have a high school senior in the house! Brace yourself for a roller-coaster of emotions, because this last year of high school is nothing short of a wild ride. However, let's keep the spotlight where it belongs—right on your incredible teen and all their accomplishments. Sure, some folks get caught up in labels such as "Most Likely to…" or in perfect GPA drama, but what truly matters is acknowledging everything your kid has pulled off. Whether this will be your first rodeo with a soon-to-be high school graduate or you're a seasoned pro, watching your student complete high school will have you bursting with pride. Let your high school senior know just how proud you are of them.

Now, buckle up for the whirlwind of activities coming your way during this epic final year. As you gear up for all the senior year shenanigans, keep in mind that too much planning can stir up some stress for your soon-to-be graduate. Speaking from more than seven years of senior experience (and surviving two high school graduations with my own kids), I've gathered a wealth of wisdom to share.

Celebrate!

The transition from junior to senior year is filled with nostalgia and anticipation. As you think back to your graduation year, you might recall the popular songs and fashion trends that defined your time as a high school senior. It's a period when you felt grown up and invincible, highlighted by amazing moments and a sense of accomplishment. This year is packed with milestone events that mark the journey from high school to whatever exciting adventures lie ahead. Help your senior cross off items on their high school bucket list, such as attending memorable class assemblies and participating in activities that scream "we made it!" It's all about celebrating their achievements and creating those "remember when" moments that'll bring a smile to their face for years to come.

As a '90s baby, I celebrated my graduation with a family dinner and cake at home, dancing to Ricky Martin's "Livin' la Vida Loca" with family and a few friends. Fast-forward to my own children's senior years, and the celebrations evolved. For my oldest, we went all out with a hotel venue, DJ, and catered spread. However, the party was shorter than expected, as the kids hopped around to other graduation celebrations. Taking this into account, my younger son opted for a smaller gathering with family and a few friends, reminiscent of my own graduation party. We set up tents, had a simple barbecue, and made floral centerpieces for everyone to take home. Reflecting on these transformations, I realize the importance of listening to my children's preferences.

Looking ahead to the end of your teen's senior year, it's never too early to start planning. Learning from my experience, early planning during the summer months before senior year can bring financial benefits. The senior year can be financially demanding, and staying ahead of the expenses, even with a budget, is crucial. Graduation cap and gown need to be purchased. Perhaps your student will want to commemorate their high school career with a graduation ring. There are companies that target your child with cool sweatshirts, lanyards, invitations, etc. They're so appealing—I want to buy them, too! Being proactive in addressing upcoming expectations ensures a smoother and more enjoyable senior year for both parents and students alike.

Plan Ahead

The nine months of the school year will fly by quickly. It's hard to imagine that within those nine months, your child will possibly turn 18 (and be a legal adult) and receive their high school diploma. Some seniors may have tentative plans, such as moving out, moving away, going to college, getting a job, or taking a gap year. All you can do as a parent or guardian is help your teen plan. And you know what they say about plans—they're always going to change, but it is nice to have a guide.

Think about how you can help your child be financially responsible and make good choices when it comes to being in charge of their own rent and utilities. Encourage your child to ask for help and look at how to prepare for the move a few months in advance. One shock I encountered when I first moved out was the cost of a security deposit on top of the first and last month's rent.

If your teen is thinking about going to college, try to schedule campus visits in the fall if you haven't begun these already. In New Mexico, we have several universities that are in close proximity to each other, which allows for campus trips that can be done in a day. Encourage your teen to fill out FAFSA, the financial aid application, even if your family feels it may not qualify. Have your teen take the SAT or ACT, especially if they are being recruited by colleges for athletics. That is one thing that recruits do ask for—the athlete's test scores. Have your teen work closely with their school counselor in preparation for what comes up after high school graduation.

For anything that your teen is interested in, encourage them to meet with an expert. If your student is interested in the military, have them start talking to a recruiter during the summer before their senior year. Many colleges, scholarship applications, and military personnel will ask about test scores, transcripts, and letters of recommendation. These may take a few months to get together, so start planning early (and read more about these preparations in chapters 8 and 9). This cannot be emphasized enough.

Encourage Participation

As your teen enters their senior year in high school, you might wonder why it's important for them to participate in social events and activities. Senior year is more than just academics; it's a transformative and memorable time. Even if your student has not participated in school sports and other extracurriculars, there is still time for self-discovery. Encourage your senior to explore new interests or join clubs or groups aligned with their passions. This not only opens up avenues for meeting like-minded individuals, but it also fosters personal growth.

All high schools are different, and the events that are planned for seniors varies, but students will receive invitations or announcements about exclusive events. These events are only for seniors, such as a senior breakfast. At our high school, the school counselors and senior sponsors organize a senior sunrise to celebrate the last sunrise they'll see as high school students. Additional events may include senior skip day and senior trips. Usually, the school staff plans these events, designed to celebrate their achievements and create lasting memories with friends.

Many schools have senior picture day for the yearbook. It is the first big moment where students realize that their high school career is coming to an end. Putting on that cap and gown for the school yearbook is exciting. Some families may also schedule a shoot with a professional photographer. These pictures are used for senior ads for the yearbook and graduation announcements. If this is something your family wants to do, get those pictures done early, even as early as the summer before senior year. These professional photo shoots are a chance for your child to shine and showcase their unique personality as they prepare for this significant milestone. It isn't necessary to break the bank. During my seven years as a yearbook adviser, I saw amazing pictures taken with a family digital camera. Budget what is best for you.

In addition to the traditional senior photo shoot, there is the coveted prom—the crown jewel of senior year. Get ready for the glitz and glamour! It's not just a dance; it's a memory-making moment. Imagine your senior dressed to the nines, surrounded by friends, dancing the night away under twinkling lights. Prom is a night of elegance, laughter, and those magical moments they'll reminisce about for the rest of their lives. They'll also have their pictures from the night as a keepsake. To some students, it's the ultimate high school event.

These events are about creating experiences that go beyond the classroom, forging friendships, and celebrating the unique journey each senior has had. Some of these moments will be talked about at reunions for decades. Encouraging your child to participate in senior traditions is like the secret sauce that makes their last year in high school extra-special. From signing yearbooks to senior pranks (the good-natured kind, of course!), these traditions create memories that will last a lifetime. It can be challenging to keep track of all the events the school has planned for seniors, so mark your calendars for senior celebrations. The year will fly by, and before you know it, you'll be watching your child walk across the stage, to receive their high school diploma.

The Importance of Friendships

Senior year is filled with milestones and traditions. Participating in social events allows your teen to create lasting memories with friends and peers. These shared experiences become cherished stories they'll carry into the future. Your high schooler has undoubtedly established friendships in school, and these social activities provide opportunities to strengthen existing friendships and forge new ones. These bonds can also serve as a support network as they navigate the transition to college or other post-high school path. I still keep in contact with the close friends I played soccer with 25 years ago. We've celebrated milestones together—babies, marriages, loves, and losses—and it is a wonderful experience to have. As your senior participates in different school events, they're developing social skills. From effective communication to teamwork, these experiences contribute to your teen's personal growth and will be valuable in college, the workforce, and beyond.

As your senior gears up for graduation, be mindful of the shifting social dynamics they might experience during this transformative time. I remember having classes as a high school senior with people I had never before seen in school, but I enjoyed talking to them. They were different from my traditional friend group. Encourage your senior to be open to forming new friendships. Graduation often brings changes in social circles, as everyone moves onto different paths. Let your senior know that it is okay to go different ways and change. Remind them that new connections can bring fresh perspectives and exciting experiences.

Keeping Balance

While academics are crucial, senior year is about creating a balance between school and fun activities. School events teach your child valuable life skills such as time management, decision-making, and the ability to navigate social situations—a balance that will serve them well in their future endeavors. By participating in school events, your teen will learn to embrace change, gain independence, and navigate the complexities of young adulthood. These experiences contribute to their personal development. Encouraging your teen to actively participate in social events during their senior year isn't just about having fun; it's an investment in their holistic growth. These experiences can help shape their character, strengthen their social connections, and create a tapestry of memories that will accompany them into the next exciting phase of life. While academics should remain a priority, senior year is a time for your child to thrive socially, emotionally, and personally. Graduating high school is a significant step toward independence. Encouraging your senior to take the initiative in social settings, whether it's making plans, reaching out to new people, or trying out different school activities, can really help your child have a memorable senior year.

This year is a time for students to blossom and experience the different academic activities at school as well. Attendance and engagement in class are more crucial than ever. They may be offered workshops, such as how to write a résumé, college preparatory sessions, financial aid assistance night (help on the FAFSA), and guidance counseling to ensure your senior finishes strong.

Closing Advice

Your senior may experience a range of emotions about leaving behind the familiar social environment of high school. Be a supportive listener, offering guidance without pushing too hard. Reassure your senior that change is a part of life, and it often brings exciting opportunities and new adventures. This year might be bittersweet for you. It's a time of letting go and allowing your senior to embrace independence. You are there to offer support, guidance, and resources to make this transition as smooth as possible.

Chapter 2
HOW IS A 12TH GRADER DIFFERENT FROM AN 11TH GRADER?

Notes on the triangular nature of education—
parents, students, and teachers

Darryl Johnson
2007 Missouri State Teacher of the Year and
2013 National Teachers Hall of Fame Inductee

My parents drove me from St. Charles, Illinois, to Maryville, Missouri, in mid-August 1987. It was my first year at Northwest Missouri State University, and I knew absolutely no one. After spending most of the day with me exploring the campus, my parents walked silently back with me in the direction of my dorm through a new parking lot adjacent to the library. An awkward, anxious feeling came over me while the gravel crunched beneath each step. I stopped, turned toward them, and looked up.

"You can go now," I stated simply.

Mom winced and started sobbing. I wasn't trying to be rude or ungrateful; I was simply ready for my new beginning, and it couldn't start with them hanging around. I hadn't seen her cry this hard in a very long time, though. Probably not since I gave her those Spider-Man Shrinky Dinks earrings for Mother's Day in 1975.

"You don't understand…" she started.

I looked at Dad. He looked as perplexed as me.

"Son," she continued, "that's *exactly* what you said to me when I dropped you off at kindergarten."

I look back at my high school experiences with moderate affection. I moved schools during 10th grade, so I had to take time to make new friends. I spent money foolishly (who doesn't need a six-foot inflatable Gumby?) and had a couple of misunderstandings with law enforcement. Life since kindergarten was calendar driven. During my senior year, like my classmates, I was so busy celebrating "the end" that I spent too little time contemplating the definition of commencement: a beginning.

The Path to Parenting Less

I once read that time is a quiet thief. To gain an amusing insight into raising children to adulthood, I encourage parents to watch poet Billy Collins perform "The Lanyard" on YouTube. The speaker of the poem, a reflective adult, encapsulates a newfound perspective of delayed appreciation and love for his mother. In his trademark wry tone, Collins understates but celebrates his upbringing and punctuates the universal understanding of sacrifice and gratitude.

Let's be clear: Being a parent of a 12th grader is both exciting and nerve-racking. After all, parents have the most important job in the world…and they're a child's first teacher. However, the stark reality is that, while we are always going to be parents to our children, we eventually must accept that we will be *parenting* less. In short, parenting well is a responsibility of epic proportions.

I grew up on the shores of Lake Michigan in Port Washington, Wisconsin. We were taught to love fishing and the Green Bay Packers. Let's look at fishing and parenting 12th graders. The fishing line connects you with that rainbow trout that wants to be free; if the angler yanks too hard on the line, it snaps and the fish "runs." However, if the angler gives the fish some slack, it'll eventually find its way home. A flawed metaphor, maybe, but as parents of 17- and 18-year-olds, we know two things: We want them to come back and spend time with the family, and deep down we know they don't have to.

Finding Their Voice

Eleventh grade, it could be argued, is much more important than 12th grade. Academically, what a student does (or doesn't) accomplish as a junior sets up much of their last year. Senior year, however it looks, can be paradoxical; it's this Venn diagram where parents and students have one foot and one eye on the present and the other foot and eye on the future. Students are both completing and commencing. The sense of nostalgia is strong, but so are visions of hope, success, and independence.

Teaching seniors for nearly 30 years has given me this insight: Most are ready for their next chapter by mid- to late-November. American schools offer lots of coming-of-age experiences—although many of these cater to extroverts. I was often assigned to sit amongst 12th graders during pep rallies. End-of-the-day assemblies have the best of intentions: to celebrate school identity and pride and foster student engagement. What I found most intriguing was observing those students who did not root during dodgeball tournaments, engage in the spirit-filled chants, or invest in class competitions. They were required to be in attendance, but these young adults understood that "popular" was not necessarily synonymous with "good." These students couldn't wait to hit the parking lot. Others more assimilated to the expectations of enhancing school culture thrived in these rallies. As a teacher, I embraced and supported it all.

I'm also a parent of children who are now in their mid-20s, so I've lived through their secondary educational experiences. Twelfth grade conjures up a flurry of emotions for parents, and it's difficult to step back and allow a child to experience their senior year with support and without too much interference from Mom and Dad. The post-COVID years have introduced an additional challenge to many parents: to help their students become less dependent and more accountable, when many young adults have spent the last few years being more dependent and less accountable. Regardless, I have enough experience as an educator and parent to understand that there is no such thing as an average person.

Further, all young adults have a voice, but, sadly, many students don't think teachers, parents, or other adults want to hear it. I had students who roared in class but squeaked on paper; I was always thrilled to have those who squeaked in class but roared on paper. Writing and speaking were the ways I heard their voices, and I firmly believed that if I was going to *teach* my students, I had to *know* and *hear* them. Scholarship and college entrance committees are drawn to voices and topics that are not necessarily cosmic or earth-shattering. I recommend students write about topics that demonstrate passion and reflection.

Enter to Learn, Learn to Serve

You may have heard the phrase: "College is for everybody, but not everybody is for college." It's not where people go beyond high school, it's what they do with the education they receive afterward.

Education is the interstate to independence.

Education is the safeguard against suppression.

Education is the antidote for apathy.

David Brooks refers to Martin Luther King, Jr., in his book *The Second Mountain*. King said your work should have length—something you get better at over a lifetime. It should have breadth—it should touch many other people. And it should have height—it should put you in service to some ideal and satisfy the soul's yearning for righteousness. I had a sign on my classroom window for all to see that read: "Enter to learn. Leave to serve." I would often allow students to opt out of a final exam in exchange for doing community outreach based on the social and community issues within the literature we studied. These young adults walked away with pride and fulfillment. Students moved from awareness to action and, in doing so, recognized their personal and collective responsibilities within their community.

I have my home serviced by HVAC experts twice a year, and the brothers who do this are former students. They are smart, professional, courteous, and driven. I also have former students who serve as mechanics, medical professionals, professors, educators, service industry members, and entrepreneurs. My daughter is a school counselor and my son serves in the Air Force.

Online Citizenry

Mark Twain once said, "If we were meant to talk more than listen, we would have two mouths and one ear." Parents should encourage their future graduates to seriously consider their presence on social media. This goes back to their voice. Many consumers of social media don't appear to be concerned with the truth. They care about what's interesting, but what's interesting isn't always true, and what's true many may not find interesting. Social media has few boundaries, and digital footprints last forever. Also, we now understand that "community" no longer simply applies to a zip code, so parents of seniors may want to warn their young adults about the perils of acting unreflectively on social media platforms. Online citizenry is a fairly new concept. Growth in the number of people who use Facebook, Instagram, X (formerly known as Twitter), Snapchat, and other social media platforms—and the time spent on them—has garnered interest and concern among policymakers, teachers, parents, and clinicians about social media's impact on our lives and psychological well-being.

Low-Risk/High-Reward Assessments

Late into the spring semester of senior year, I used to ask students to share their "coming of age" experiences. I asked for the following in a PowerPoint, Prezi, or Google Slides format, including pictures:

1. What are 10 words that best describe your middle school years?
2. What are 10 words that best describe your high school years?
3. Explain two moments of elation in your life.
4. Explain two moments of sorrow in your life.
5. Describe two formative experiences you've had since middle school/junior high.
6. Describe two important decisions you've made since middle school/junior high.
7. List five people who've impacted your life in a profound way (this doesn't have to be positive).
8. Comment on your spiritual development (or lack thereof).

9. Comment on your intellectual development.

10. List and explain two quotes that are meaningful to you.

I modeled this assessment by sharing my own and, with some vulnerability, demonstrated what my goal was with them—to reinforce empathy and community within a group of people about to start a new journey. These presentations, I have been told, have been shown on repeat during students' graduation celebrations. What a gift! Like anything else, the more students put into these reflections, the more they get out of it. You can use these activities as a way to further connect with your 12th grader.

Another formative assessment I used during students' 12th-grade year is called "Soundtrack of Your Life." Everybody loves music. Everybody attaches songs to certain times and experiences in their lives that serve as memory triggers. I would ask my seniors to list 10 songs that map out their lives, from childhood to present, and explain why each song stays with them. I also asked that they title their playlists. As usual, I modeled this before they started. My playlist is called Prozac in a Pez Dispenser: One Man's Journey Through Music. Tracks include "Free to Be…You and Me" by Marlo Thomas and Friends (early childhood memory), "Keep On Loving You" by REO Speedwagon (first dance with my middle school crush), anything from Van Halen and KISS (high school memories hanging with friends), "Love Shack" by the B-52s (college social gatherings), and "Gettin' Jiggy Wit It" by Will Smith (memory of my first snow day as a teacher and watching my baby daughter bounce to its beat in her Exersaucer).

Nearly all students completed this low-risk/high-reward activity, and when they were shared out loud, it connected the class, as the students had many of the same childhood influences. It increased engagement, strengthened community within the class, and offered a unique time line of their lives to that point. Asking parents to do this would make the experience even more enriching. At its best, it could bond families, open up communication about parent histories, and hopefully teach empathy and perspective.

The Power of One

NBC reported in February 2023 that only 43% of Americans approved of secondary and higher education. While that cuts me deeply, I continue to firmly believe that the triangular nature of education—parents, students, and teachers—remains the formula for preparing older teens for success beyond high school.

I look back at my high school experiences with lukewarmish affection. Yes, I learned much about familial, social, and workplace relationships. Yes, I was trying to learn how I learned. Yes, I exploited my parents' trust sometimes. And no, I wasn't confident in my near future.

It was an early and dark February morning in 1987 when my mother stopped me in the kitchen of our suburban Chicago home—just months before I was going to say *hasta la vista* to St. Charles High School. Before I opened the refrigerator, she clutched my right shoulder. Somewhere between a tug and a hug, she pulled me back and squared up with me.

"Son, I want to talk to you."

I'm sure my demeanor was one of exasperation and irritability. By then, I had hit my growth spurt, so I found myself looking down at her. At the time, I considered my patience and attention to hear her request a gift from my generous self.

"I've been doing a lot of thinking lately," she said. "Your brothers made their decisions to join the Air Force, and those choices served them well. We're proud of them. And it would be good for you, too. I just…well…I think you should consider going to college. You know, break the cycle. Think about it. You can do it. Be the first one in our entire family to get a college degree."

Half-offended and fully dismissive, I decided it would be in my best immediate interest to restructure the look on my face to match the intense nature and seriousness of her suggestion. Her eyes and proposal had me pinned to the refrigerator door. I would have been lying to her if I said I hadn't considered it, but I knew money was an enormous issue, not to mention the fact that I did little in high school to prepare me for such a profound change of course. My 12th-grade year consisted of taking classes such as Exploring Foods I, Advanced PE, Introduction to Business Writing, and two study halls. I skipped some classes more than others, and my priorities included working in the toy department at KMart, dating a bit, and running around with friends. College was simply a hollow idea to me at the time.

But I took a few enormous risks: I took the ACT, applied to one college, and eventually walked through the proverbial desert and found my way.

My mom passed away five years before I was named Missouri Teacher of the Year. She never got to see the fruits of her encouragement, which brings me to this: the Power of One. One person. One conversation. One moment. One nugget of encouragement can change an impressionable young adult.

Closing Advice

Let's move forward with diligence and nurture our kids with positivity and purpose, because together we can feed their growth mindset, encourage them to expect more from themselves, and convince them they are relevant to our world. You might have your 12th grader establish a free FutureMe account (futureme.org). Here, young adults (and parents) can write an email to their future selves, as long as they keep the same email account. This email response can be received from five months to 10 years from when it's sent. This resource could be a reflective treasure in the development of a young adult.

Years ago, I had a student named Andy in class. He must have liked me a lot, because he took my sophomore English class three times. Anyway, he said something one day that has become one of the pillars of my teaching philosophy: "If they [teachers] don't care about teaching, I see no reason to prove to them that I care about learning." It was a mammoth insight for me, and this idea is easily translatable to parenting.

Before my 12th graders left me at the end of the year—and it was a challenge to retain their attention in late spring—I sat among them and offered these words:

1. Represent yourself well.
2. Represent your family well.
3. Be faithful to your dreams.
4. And never abandon the child within.

And we all carry on.

Chapter 3
CHOOSING CLASSES

How to understand your student's course selections

Mary Lou Mendoza
High School Counselor, New Mexico

In the words of the Pink Ladies in *Grease*, "This time, we're seniors. And we're gonna rule the school!" I don't know about you, but that was my thinking when I entered my senior year, along with: "It's going to be a breeze! I've worked hard and come this far, so I deserve to take it easy!" That was definitely not the case. My senior year was an emotional roller coaster because, not only was I relieved and excited by the fact that I was almost at the finish line, but also the fear and stress of "Oh shoot, what am I going to do now?" set in.

Your senior is also going to experience a mix of emotions, especially because there are going to be a lot of lasts this year: last first day of school, last prom, and the last time they will select their high school courses. Such bittersweet moments. Throughout their years in high school, students are given the responsibility to make important academic decisions that can have an impact on their future goals. This chapter will cover some of the things you should be aware of when helping your high school senior select their courses.

Core Classes

Your student and their school counselor will create a schedule based on the core classes that are still needed for graduation and in preparation for the future. Graduation requirements vary from state to state, but most colleges require that a student has completed four years of English, four years of math, three to four years of history, three to four years of science, and a minimum of two years of a foreign language, including electives and AP or honors courses (see more about AP on page 22).

The course selection process also varies from school to school, but communication is key with all parties involved. Your student should have an open dialogue with their school counselor to help identify your student's likes, dislikes, strengths, weaknesses, and goals for the future. You can also play an active role prior to course selection by providing a listening ear and engaging in conversation. Ask your teen questions and listen to their plans for the future. Here are just a few questions you can ask your teen to help them select their courses:

1. What do you want to do when you graduate from high school?
2. What are you passionate about?
3. If you have chosen the college route, what courses do they require?
4. Have the courses you selected helped with your college/scholarship applications?

While you can offer guidance and support, the final decision on course selection should be your teen's. Trust that they chose the best courses for themselves. This will not only foster confidence and responsibility, but also a positive learning experience.

Electives

One way to discover your student's interests and strengths is through elective courses, which are usually required as a part of the graduation requirements but are not a part of the core curriculum. Some examples of elective courses include art, theater, technology, journalism, and dance. The number of electives that can be taken each year in high school varies depending on how many fit into the schedule once the core classes that are needed for graduation have been added. In most circumstances, seniors can take more electives than underclassmen, because most of the courses needed for graduation have been completed by the time they reach their final year of high school. Review the course catalog, which can usually be found on your school's website.

Some electives may not add as much to your student's workload as an academic course would. This is why taking a class that your teen finds fun and interesting can give them something to look forward to during the school day and make the day more enjoyable. Some students will take elective courses just to be with their friends, and that's okay. Elective classes can encourage students to stay motivated in their final year of high school, especially when senioritis kicks in (see Chapter 11 for more about the Senior Slump).

Some electives, such as band and dance, may involve extracurricular activities that require your student to put in more hours during the school day or on weekends. The benefits of extracurricular activities, though, is that they encourage students to manage their time and work harder to attain better grades, attend school on a regular basis, and feel a sense of community. Extracurricular activities are not required for graduation, but they're a great way to get teens involved in things they are passionate about and can also be mentioned in college applications.

Choosing electives based on your teen's strengths and interests helps them gain experience. Many colleges like to see applicants who are already taking steps toward career goals. For example, a student who is interested in studying to become an engineer should consider taking electives such as Intro to Engineering alongside AP core math and science courses.

Advanced Placement (AP) and Honors Courses

The AP program, run by the College Board, gives students the opportunity to take college-level courses while they are still in high school and receive college credit if they score well on the AP test (a 3 out of 5 means they passed, though some colleges require at least a 4). This means that they can begin college with a head start on credits and the ability to finish early. Most importantly, it can save you some money on tuition. College Board is such a helpful tool if you and your teen are having a difficult time deciding what AP courses they should take. The College Board makes recommendations based on performance on its PSAT/SAT assessment. Students can review this information by logging into their College Board account and reviewing their score report. The score report will list all AP courses your high schooler might do well in based on their test scores.

One benefit of taking AP classes is that it can help students boost their GPA, as they often add one point to the grade. For example, an A in an AP math class would be worth five points as opposed to four points in a regular math class. This boost can improve students' rankings. Students who are interested in graduating at the top of their class should consider taking AP classes.

AP courses are more rigorous and demanding than regular courses. Therefore, it is important for students and parents to know that taking an AP class involves great commitment to the coursework and the AP exam. Yet these AP courses will help students develop the knowledge and skills necessary for a successful transition to college. Also, it increases a student's confidence that they can do college-level work.

Honors courses are also academically challenging and move at a faster pace. They are open to students who maintain an average grade of B or higher in a similar class. Honors classes vary greatly in design and content depending on the school your student attends. While these courses are academically challenging, AP courses are more academically rigorous. The primary difference between honors and AP is that AP courses can result in college credit. Students do not get college credit for completing honors courses, but they are designed for students who want an academic challenge. Just like AP courses, honors courses give students a chance to boost their grade point average. In many high schools, honors classes are assigned an additional 0.5 grade point. This will benefit your student with regard to class rankings and scholarships.

Many colleges offer merit scholarships for students based on their GPA, so taking an AP or honors course could get your student closer to qualifying for these awards. Merit-based scholarships are given to students who excel in academics, athletics, arts, or other areas of special interest. Merit aid is often provided by colleges and universities and can be redeemed for multiple semesters or years. Unlike student loans that you have to pay back, merit scholarships provide college students with free money to help pay for school and other expenses, regardless of their financial status.

Your teen's decision to take an honors course or an AP course mostly comes down to their goals. If they are simply looking for a more challenging academic experience, honors classes are the right choice. However, if they want college credit on top of that, AP is the way to go. Ask your student what they think they can handle. They should never sign up for more honors or AP courses than they can handle, especially if they already have a busy schedule with extracurricular activities. Trying to do too much at once and getting low grades can look bad on college applications, so help your teen maintain a well-balanced schedule.

Dual Credit

Some schools offer dual-credit courses that can also help a student receive college credit and increase their GPA. The Dual Credit (DC) Program in New Mexico, for example, provides academic credit simultaneously while a student attends both a high school and a college/university. While some students take basic DC courses such as English and math, other DC coursework may include subjects such as criminal justice or psychology, depending on what the postsecondary institution has to offer. Academic adviser from the postsecondary institution will advise students interested in taking DC courses based on their interests and goals.

If your teen's schedule has some openings, they should consider taking DC courses. This might be one or two semester courses in the fall and then one or two semester courses again in the spring, depending on your school's policy. One thing to keep in mind is that DC courses are more demanding than regular courses because they are college-level courses. Ask your student if they feel prepared to fully commit themselves to doing well on their college coursework, because failing these courses could affect their financial aid offer and college GPA. On the bright side, the benefit of taking a college course will keep your student challenged, prepare them for college, and give them college credits.

Career and Technical Courses

Career and technical education, also known as CTE, teaches specific career skills to high school students. CTE pathways offer hands-on, real-world learning experiences, allowing students to gain experience in a chosen field, which could help with college or career readiness. CTE programs may be offered in agriculture, engineering, business, and hospitality, among other career areas. CTE allows students to shadow knowledgeable teachers and gain hands-on experience, along with certifications that demonstrate mastery over specific topics. CTE courses also look good on college applications. It shows the university that your child is planning to pursue their education in that field. CTE also serves students who will not or are not ready to attend a college/university. Many students who have completed CTE programs are employable right after high school graduation because they do have this hands-on experience.

Is your teen passionate about cars or baking? Do they have a skill set for science or communication? Ask your teenager questions to help them determine what kind of program might match their abilities.

Students with Disabilities

The vast majority of students with disabilities have an Individualized Education Program (IEP). The student's IEP identifies their strengths and needs, academic goals, and accommodations necessary to support success with the academic coursework. An IEP facilitator or the student's case manager can help support decisions surrounding course selection. If you are a parent of a student with a disability, ask questions regarding course selection during your IEP meeting because graduation requirements vary from state to state.

Closing Advice

It is important that students do well in their final year of high school. You can encourage your high schooler to pick their classes for the coming year with the goal to challenge, but not overwhelm, them, and trust that they have made the best decision for themselves. There will be times when your student will feel anxious, overwhelmed, and scared, so help them find a good balance so they can work hard but also take time to enjoy the special moments of senior year. Remember that high school counselors are there to support you, too.

S.E.N.I.O.R.

One of the common misconceptions that students have is that the senior year should be the easiest—but it is definitely not. It's so important to talk to your senior about how they can, and should, make this a year that matters. Here are some reminders for helping your student with course selection based on their strengths, interests, and plans for the future:

Support: Trust that your student has chosen the best courses. While you can offer guidance, the final decision should be theirs.

Encourage: Nudge your student to select courses that can help their college admissions application and increase their GPA (if that's their path forward).

Navigate: Help your senior navigate the final year of high school. It might be a roller coaster, but enjoy the ride.

Identify: List what your teen excels at and is passionate about and encourage them to take courses that match those interests.

Open up: Ask your teen questions and listen to them. Good communication can help ensure that they make the best decisions for their future.

Reward: Reward yourself and your senior in whatever way you'd like, because you've earned it!

Chapter 4
INCLUSION

How to support your student's identity, safety, and allyship

Shari Collins
Educational Consultant, Nebraska

When you were in high school, do you remember trying to fit in and feel included? Do you remember trying to find your way? Who would you sit with if your closest friends weren't at school that day? Where were the safe spaces where you felt supported? Who could you go to for help? If you were having a crisis, who would help you? Did you ever think, "How do I make new friends?"

These are some of the same questions your 12th grader may be asking as they think about inclusion. How can you support your student as they wrap up their high school career and begin thinking about a new adventure outside of the K–12 school setting?

What is inclusion, anyway? According to the Oxford Dictionary, inclusion is "the action or state of including or of being included within a group or structure." As an educator for more than 40 years, I define inclusion as "recognizing and appreciating your own various skills, talents, and identities, as well as being aware of other people's skills, talents, and identities." It's about being seen and heard for your own uniqueness and being aware of others'.

Identity

When we talk about inclusion, we must include identities. Maybe your teen hasn't really thought about all the pieces of someone's background that comprise an individual. These identities can include many things, such as age, faith, life experiences, religion, language, gender, family structure, education, socioeconomic status, and more. As your student's world becomes bigger as they finish their K–12 education, you might ask your senior:

- How many people does our family know who hold differing identities?
- How can we uplift these differences with empathy and kindness?
- Do we have bias toward those individuals who hold different identities than we have? If so, what are these biases?
- Have we researched other identities so we have some understanding and awareness around identities that our family doesn't hold?
- What can we do in our family and our community to support those who are different from us?
- What can we do as parents to help you feel included?
- What do your friends do to include you?

If your teen is attending a college or going into the workforce, follow their social media sites and check out their websites. They may have inclusive programming in place that your student can join.

Safety

The U.S. Department of Education opens its March 2023 report, *Guiding Principles for Creating Safe, Inclusive, Supportive, and Fair School Climates*, with the statement, "All students deserve learning environments that are safe, inclusive, supportive, and fair. Schools can both keep their school community—including students and school staff—safe while ensuring every student is included, supported, and treated fairly." This quote is meaningful to me, both as an educator and a parent. With inclusion comes the ideas of *safety, support*, and *fairness*. How can we help to ensure safety for our students? Without being helicopter parents, what support networks can we uphold?

Set up an environment where the child can fail. Yes, I said, "fail." We learn from our mistakes, so we have to be comfortable trying new things. Are you modeling that behavior? Do you admit your mistakes? Are you willing to try new things? Your student is watching you, even as they near adulthood, and witnessing your mindset. Make your home a safe space for mistakes. If you are interested in learning more about fixed mindsets versus growth mindsets, a great read is Carol Dweck's 2006 book, *Mindset: The New Psychology of Success*. Growth and development can flourish in a growth mindset where we can safely make mistakes and learn.

Ensure physical and emotional safety at school, the workplace, and in the home. As an educator who has studied bullying for decades, I bring up the difference between inclusionary and exclusionary behaviors. Ask your student to think of a time when they remember being included versus a time when they were excluded. When we think of bullying, often we think of overt tactics of force and power. However, students can also be bullied covertly, through exclusion. This can occur in a variety of ways, such as being repeatedly isolated, having important information withheld, not being invited to events, and being excluded from group chats electronically. Think of the movie *Mean Girls* if you want to see bullying in action. In fact, this could be a family activity. Watch the movie together, identify exclusionary tactics, and strategize what your student could do to create inclusion. Don't think this is just for girls, as boys can learn how to be upstanders, as well. If your child sees bullying and exclusion in their school environment, please encourage them to seek out the anti-bullying educator in the building, school psychologist, or their school counselor.

Did you know the brain registers social rejection from exclusion as pain? Social pain activates the same regions in the brain as physical pain. In 2003, social psychologist Naomi Eisenberger from the University of California, Los Angeles, used magnetic resonance images to monitor brain activity around social rejection. The study showed the need for connectedness with others, as the anterior cingulate cortex that responds to physical pain also responded to social pain. Why does this matter? If your student has headaches, stomachaches, or other pain, ask if they feel they are being excluded. You might be surprised by the answers you get.

Allyship

What is an ally? Cambridge Dictionary defines an ally as "someone who helps and supports other people who are part of a group that is treated badly or unfairly, although they are not themselves a member of this group." Allyship is an opportunity to support inclusion through our actions. By developing positive peer relationships through clubs and socialization, your student can find situations to demonstrate allyship. By encouraging positive words and attitudes toward diversity at home and positive views of education you can model allyship.

Here are some questions to get your senior thinking about opportunities to show allyship and inclusion:

- Do you model inclusive behavior at school, not just with words but also through actions?
- What inclusive behaviors do your teachers use? How are they allies?
- How do you support others' voices when they aren't in the room?
- How do you uplift peers of other identities who may need support?
- Are you a mentor? When? How?
- Are you a coach? When? How?
- Are you an upstander? When? How?
- How will you step in and speak up if you see/hear something that's wrong?
- Do you ask if you are pronouncing someone's name correctly?
- Do you ask about preferred pronouns so you don't misgender anyone?
- How do you demonstrate empathy for others?

Change

As a 12th-grade parent, many parts of your life and your student's life are about to change. Whether your student is college-bound, heading to the trades, taking a gap year, or going into the workforce, there will be changes across all your systems. You've set the foundation; now it's time to embrace the new experiences. With change, there can be stress and anxiety. Find ways together to alleviate your stress. Try "nature bathing" and being outdoors. Take a walk, enjoy the birds, plant flowers. Research shows that by spending 20 minutes in nature, cortisol levels drop. Find positive psychology hacks to lift your positivity. Show gratitude. Listen to music without lyrics. Smile. Embrace the changes. Find hope.

Hope

Hope is a powerful tool that provides several pathways to future success. According to International School psychologist Dr. Alysha Collins in her thesis, *Hope in the Time of Crisis*, fostering hope is vital. When students realize that the future will be better than the present, it is hope in action. Dr. Collins writes, "Hope can continue to help alleviate…difficulties that arise in the future. To invest in hopeful educational staff, we invest in the future of our youth." When everyone is inclusive, from educators to parents to students, it will make our world a more hopeful place.

Mental Health

Our moods, behaviors, and actions can impact how we handle stress, social situations, relationships, and how we show up at work or school. Are we inclusive of those with mental health issues? What if you or your child experiences a mental health crisis? Do you have a plan of attack? Who are the people in your mental health support system? Will your child need extra support after high school in academic, social, or medical areas? Do you have plans determined for these areas? The mental health crisis line, available in English and Spanish, is open 24/7 by calling 988. Please share this number widely within your circles.

Closing Advice

Inclusive settings set us all up for success and growth. Keep the lines of communication open and collaborate with school personnel as needed. Continue to learn about those different from your family unit. Train your brain to find positivity in each day. Discuss what brings you joy and how you can amplify those moments. Celebrate your strengths, as well as your child's strengths, and what makes everyone unique. Finally, be kind.

> **Conversation Starters**
>
> In all conversations with your teen, listen to learn. Listen to understand, not to respond. Ask open-ended questions so you can hear your teen's thoughts. Limit knee-jerk responses, and try to reflect and be curious. What answers will your student provide to the questions I posed in the introductory paragraph of this chapter?
>
> - What are you doing to fit in and feel included?
> - How are you trying to find your way?
> - Who would you sit with if your closest friends weren't at school that day?
> - Where are your safe spaces, and where do you feel supported?
> - Who do you go to for help?
> - If you are having a crisis, who would help you?
> - How do you make new friends?

Chapter 5
BUILDING STUDY SKILLS

How to support your student in taking
ownership of their learning

Al Rabanera
High School Algebra Teacher, California

College or career...ready? As Brandon began his final chapter of high school, the decisions that he would make during his senior year would directly impact his next steps after walking across the graduation stage to receive his diploma. As students like Brandon approached the end of their senior school year, it was important to me to teach them how to develop and refine their ability to plan, implement, and be self-reflective about their own learning. These skills are essential, because they allow students to apply their abilities, knowledge, and experiences across different situations, roles, and future careers.

Setting High Expectations and Providing a Supportive Environment

At the beginning of each year, my students and I participate in icebreaker activities so that we can get to know each other before we dive into the academic content. From one of these activities, I learned that Brandon needed to be given clear and concise directions so that he would be successful in class.

I like to talk with my students about having high expectations and the importance of personal accountability. I model what high expectations and accountability look and sound like. With the proper classroom engagement and motivation, students rise to and oftentimes surpass the expectations set in class. I teach my students about the importance of being able to self-monitor their learning and understanding of content. In postsecondary educational settings and in the workforce, being able to learn, assess, and adapt are crucial skills.

You can also explicitly model how to communicate high expectations for yourself and for your teen at home. This strategy can help shape and reinforce your student's independent study skills. Encourage your teen to meet the high expectations at home by:

- Being clear about your expectations and setting goals
- Providing support so your teen maintains motivation to focus on meeting those goals
- Providing opportunities to practice time management

Although high expectations may already be in place at home, show yourself and your teen grace when mistakes are made and expectations are not met. A way to maintain and revisit high expectations is to establish routines to provide structure and predictability that your student will be able to replicate in different settings to enhance their focus and concentration.

Establish a routine

Building a study routine is one of the most effective ways to boost your student's academic performance. It provides structure, consistency, and focus, leading to better understanding and retention of information. By setting clear goals and breaking them down into smaller, manageable tasks, I was able to help Brandon prioritize his work, helping him to remain focused.

At home, establishing routines takes the guesswork out of what your student can do next to self-monitor their learning and study habits. Routines can increase productivity by creating a habitual environment for your student to work and, over time, can lead to an increase in consistency and a sense of stability. To support your student developing essential learning habits at home:

- Create a dedicated study space.
- Establish a regular study schedule.
- Start small and stay consistent.
- Celebrate learning wins.

Promote effective time management

As the school year moved forward, each time I checked in with Brandon I could tell that he was becoming overwhelmed because he felt like he was falling behind in class. Brandon seemed disconnected and distracted more frequently as the school year progressed. To help Brandon mitigate these feelings, we had a conversation to help him name what he was feeling, what was contributing to that feeling, and what he could do differently to help him overcome the feeling of being overwhelmed. Brandon came to the conclusion that the best way for him to help himself was to prioritize his time-management skills. The time-management strategies that I shared with Brandon were to break down the larger tasks into smaller, more manageable chunks, so he could experience small wins to help him build his self-confidence. By prioritizing tasks, Brandon was able to organize himself, so rather than being overwhelmed, he was being more efficient with his time as he completed tasks.

How can you be proactive to help your student mitigate procrastination, which can lead to the feeling of being overwhelmed? Give your teen opportunities to practice their time-management skills. The more practice that students have managing their time, the more likely they will be more effective in completing tasks in the long term. Time-management skills are essential for all aspects of life and can yield countless benefits for your young adult in present and future tasks and situations, ultimately impacting their success. Time management is a beneficial transferable life skill that can be applied to many areas of your teen's life. By incorporating time-management skills into their daily routines, your student will be equipped with a strategy to help them navigate challenges that come up in life. Some strategies to support your student with time-management skills are:

- Helping estimate the time needed for each task
- Teaching prioritization skills
- Using time-management tools like schedules, planners, and timers

Foster Independence and Responsibility

Knowing that Brandon needed support with his time-management skills, I checked in on him regularly. I also gave him space so he did not feel like I was hovering over him, but rather encouraging and motivating him like a coach with an athlete. The check-ins with Brandon were more to see how he was feeling and to remind him that I was there to support him and provide him with guidance when he asked.

Supporting the gradual reduction of your involvement in your student's homework and study skills helps them become an independent learner. The development of independence and responsibility can encourage your student to employ their critical thinking and problem-solving skills. This is crucial for preparing your student for the academic rigors of college, the employability skills of a career, and the general challenges of adulthood. Here are some strategies to help foster independence:

- Provide resources and tools to support your student's cognitive, social, and emotional development.
- Guide your student; refrain from solving the challenge in front of them.
- Teach time management (see page 39).

Teach problem-solving skills

As the school year progressed, I knew it was crucial to not only teach Brandon how to identify when to use his problem-solving skills, but also to provide him opportunities to practice using those skills as a way to build up his confidence. I started asking open-ended questions about how he was doing and then moved the conversation to his academics, being mindful to provide Brandon with opportunities to be reflective about his decision-making processes.

Teaching problem-solving skills at home is a valuable way to support and reinforce your teen's academic success. Be mindful that there may be more than one way to solve problems, and it is important for your student to recognize at times that there is no immediate solution to solving a problem. It is also important to demonstrate how you approach and solve problems in your own life. It is beneficial for your child to know and understand your steps and thought processes when you make decisions and how you handle challenges.

Some strategies that you can use to teach problem-solving skills at home are:

- Encouraging your child to think critically
- Asking guiding questions to help them work through challenges independently
- Providing a supportive environment
- Modeling your own decision-making

Self-directed learning

An instructional strategy that I use to help students make learning their own is the "I Do, We Do, You Do" method. I start with the "I Do" step and make sure that I have all my students' attention. I then model what I would like my students to do during the lesson. The next step is for the class to use the exact same process to problem-solve another example. During the "We Do" process, I ask students questions to check for understanding, to provide guidance when students have challenges, and to share common errors to avoid. This step was especially helpful for Brandon, because it gave him an opportunity to practice the skill that I wanted the class to learn—the gradual release of responsibility, shifting to the "You Do" step. During the "You Do" step, my students are problem-solving independently.

To support self-directed learning at home, couple it with the idea of a growth mindset. A growth mindset is a way of thinking that emphasizes the potential for development and improvement. It is based on the belief that our abilities and intelligences are not fixed, but rather fluid and capable of expanding through effort and dedication. By encouraging your student to develop a growth mindset, you teach your child that intelligence and abilities can be developed through effort and perseverance and that there is value in learning from mistakes. Support your student in:

- Learning from mistakes
- Persisting despite difficulties
- Finding joy in the learning process

Gradually Reduce Involvement

Each of my students needs a different type of support to be successful. Knowing that each of my students learns differently, I leverage their learning style and strengths when I check their understanding during a lesson and adjust my approach to meet their individual needs. What works for one of my students may not be the best approach for another, so I am mindful to be flexible and adaptable.

Remember that patience is key, and allow your teen time to develop their independent study skills. It may be difficult to gradually reduce your involvement in your student's academic choices. Just know that there will be stumbles and setbacks as a natural part of the learning process, but also remember that it is equally important to celebrate your teen's progress. Even if they approach working through challenges differently than you would, offer constructive feedback instead of criticism. Some strategies that you can use at home to gradually reduce your involvement as a parent are:

- Cultivate your teen's confidence in making decisions.
- Respect the choices that your student makes.
- Avoid comparisons.
- Trust and believe in your soon-to-be adult.

Encourage self-management

Brandon's self-confidence increased as the school year progressed, and so did his ability to self-manage and reflect upon his academic progress. The check-in conversations that I had with Brandon shifted from how to organize his time and setting small achievable goals at the beginning of the year to how to adapt to change and reflect on his learning progress. I started asking Brandon questions about how *he* best felt that I could continue to support his learning needs and goals. This shift encouraged Brandon to think about better understanding his learning processes.

Be mindful in the development of your student's self-management that it is a collaborative journey. By providing your teen with opportunities to practice their self-management skills, you are letting them experience the natural consequences of their choices, both positive and negative. You can provide a safe and supportive environment for your student to make these choices by offering guidance as they become more independent as a learner and as their own unique person. A few strategies you can use to encourage your student to develop their self-management skills are:

- Offering positive reinforcement
- Providing opportunities for your child to make decisions
- Being patient and supportive

Closing Advice

As your student enters senior year, it becomes increasingly important that they continue to develop their independent study skills as they prepare to become college or career ready. Some reflective questions you can ask yourself about how you can help your student in constructive ways are:

- What are the different ways to set high expectations for my student?
- What are different ways to provide my student with a supportive learning environment?
- What types of routines would work best for my student?
- What are different ways to help my student with time management?
- What are different ways to help my student cultivate their self-confidence?

Chapter 6
OVERCOMING ACADEMIC SETBACKS

How to help your 12th grader with resilience, self-reflection, and independence

Antoine Sharpe
2020 Department of Defense Teacher of the Year

Picture this: It's another school evening, and you're sitting across from your high school senior who's just experienced a setback—maybe a failed quiz, a stumble during a class presentation, or a forgotten assignment. As a parent, it's natural to feel a twinge of worry and maybe even a desire to fix things. But what if I told you that these moments, uncomfortable as they are, hold the key to some of life's most valuable lessons? Let's explore how we can turn these setbacks into stepping stones for growth.

This chapter isn't just about coping with academic disappointments; it's a blueprint for building resilience. It's about understanding why these setbacks are not just inevitable, but also invaluable in preparing our teens for the world beyond high school. We'll delve into strategies and conversations that can transform these experiences from sources of stress into opportunities for learning and empowerment. Here, we unravel the art of turning defeats into victories.

Understanding Resilience

Resilience is the ability to bounce back from setbacks, adapt in the face of adversity, and emerge stronger from the experience. It's a skill that goes beyond merely recovering from a difficulty; it involves developing the capacity to learn from challenges and use them as a springboard for growth. Students who cultivate resilience are better prepared to handle the complexities and pressures of adult life, including college and career challenges and personal adversities.

For a high school senior nearing graduation, the development of resilience is especially crucial. Graduation marks the transition from a structured school environment to the more unpredictable landscape of adult life. Educational research underscores how a student's mindset can significantly influence their learning and personal development. A positive, growth-oriented mindset sees challenges as chances to improve and learn, while a fixed mindset may view them as insurmountable barriers. To illustrate this concept in a more relatable context, let's consider an example of a positive interaction between a parent and a student facing a setback.

Dennis and Giuliana: A Case Study in Building Resilience

Meet Dennis and his daughter, Giuliana, a high school senior. Giuliana, who generally excels in school, recently failed an important math quiz. Understandably, this failure was a source of stress and disappointment for both Giuliana and Dennis. However, Dennis recognized this as a pivotal moment for teaching resilience.

Embracing empathetic listening

When Dennis approached Giuliana, his focus was on empathy instead of immediately trying to fix the problem or dismissing her feelings. He understood that the first step in helping Giuliana was to listen to her perspective and acknowledge her emotions. Dennis started their conversation with **empathetic listening**, a crucial aspect of effective communication between parents and children, especially during challenging times.

Empathetic listening involves more than just hearing the words; it's about understanding the emotions behind them. Dennis gave Giuliana his full attention, nodding and responding in a way that showed he was engaged in what she was saying. He refrained from interrupting or rushing to give advice, which can often feel dismissive. Instead, he let Giuliana fully express her feelings about the failed quiz and the disappointment that came with it.

This approach helped Giuliana feel heard and validated. It's essential for children, especially teenagers, to know that their feelings are acknowledged and taken seriously. Dennis's empathetic listening provided a safe and supportive space for Giuliana to open up. It also set the stage for a more productive conversation about how to address the setback, as it helped Giuliana understand that experiencing setbacks is a normal part of the learning process.

By starting the conversation with empathy, Dennis was able to help Giuliana approach her setback from a place of understanding and readiness to learn from the experience. This kind of supportive interaction is crucial in helping children develop resilience and the ability to overcome challenges.

Fostering self-reflection

After listening empathetically to Giuliana, Dennis asked open-ended questions like, "What do you think led to the challenges you faced in this quiz? Were there topics you found particularly hard?" This line of questioning was designed to help Giuliana critically examine the situation, even if she initially felt unsure about the answers.

Such questioning serves multiple purposes. First, it encourages the teen to think about the problem in a structured way, breaking it down into more manageable parts. By considering specific topics or questions that were challenging, Giuliana can identify her areas of weakness. Second, this approach empowers the teen to take ownership of their learning process. It prompts the teen to think about possible strategies they can use to improve. If Giuliana recognizes struggling with a particular math concept, the next logical step is to review that area more thoroughly, seek additional resources, or ask for help in that specific topic. Lastly, this questioning helps develop problem-solving skills by guiding someone to become an independent thinker and learner. By navigating through thoughts and feelings about the setback, a person learns valuable skills in analysis, decision-making, and self-evaluation. This method of guiding, rather than directing, is an effective way for parents to help their children build resilience and independence.

Harnessing positive reinforcement

By reminding Giuliana that, "One test doesn't define you. You've done well in other areas, and I'm confident you can overcome this challenge," Dennis was doing more than just offering words of encouragement. He was actively helping to shift Giuliana's perspective on the situation, a key aspect of building resilience. Positive reinforcement is a powerful tool in shaping behavior and mindset. In the context of dealing with setbacks, it serves several important functions:

1. **Shifts focus from negative to positive:** By highlighting Giuliana's past successes and strengths, Dennis redirected her attention to her capabilities as a student. This shift in focus helps counteract the tunnel vision that often accompanies failure, where one setback can feel all-consuming and defining.

2. **Encourages a growth mindset:** Reminding Giuliana that she is not defined by a single failure encourages a growth mindset—the belief that abilities and intelligence can be developed through dedication and hard work. This mindset is crucial for resilience, as it motivates individuals to learn from setbacks and view them as opportunities for growth.

3. **Builds self-efficacy:** Dennis's confidence in Giuliana's ability to overcome challenges helps build her self-efficacy—her belief in her own ability to succeed. High self-efficacy has been linked to greater motivation, perseverance, and resilience in the face of difficulties.

4. **Reduces fear of failure:** By downplaying the finality of the setback, Dennis helps reduce Giuliana's fear of failure. This is important, because fear of failure can be paralyzing, preventing students from taking risks and trying new strategies.

5. **Strengthens the parent-child bond:** Positive reinforcement in such situations also strengthens the trust and bond between parent and child. It reassures the child that they are supported and valued beyond their academic performance, which is crucial for their emotional and psychological well-being.

Nurturing independence

As the conversation ended, Dennis offered a suggestion that skillfully balanced support with encouragement for Giuliana's independence. He said, "I'm here for you if you need help. Perhaps you could talk to your teacher about this quiz, or we can look together for some extra resources to help you practice?" This was a gentle nudge for Giuliana to take the lead in addressing her academic challenge. By suggesting that his daughter might speak with her teacher, he was subtly shifting the responsibility to her, fostering her autonomy. It was an invitation for her to engage actively in finding a solution, rather than passively receiving one.

Dennis's role as a parent was to be there to support and guide but not to take over. This delicate balance is crucial in nurturing a child's independence and resilience. It teaches them that, while support is always available, the initiative to act and the power to overcome challenges lies within them.

From Narrative to Practice

To translate the essence of Dennis and Giuliana's experience into actionable steps, the following guide offers parents a structured approach. Each step is designed to help you effectively navigate these challenging moments with your teen, fostering growth, resilience, and independence.

1. **Start with Empathetic Listening**

   Listen empathetically when your teen discusses a setback.

   - *Purpose:* To create an environment of trust and understanding, making it easier for your teen to open up about their challenges.
   - *Why It's Important:* This shows your teenager that their feelings are valid and creates a safe space for them to express themselves, ensuring they feel heard and supported.
   - *Outcome:* A stronger emotional connection and a foundation for further constructive conversation.

2. **Encourage Self-Reflection**

   Ask open-ended questions.

   - *Purpose:* To develop your teenager's critical thinking and problem-solving skills.
   - *Why It's Important:* Self-reflection is vital, as it helps your teen understand what led to the setback and recognize

areas that need improvement, enabling them to independently analyze and learn from their experiences.

- *Outcome:* Enhanced self-awareness and an improved approach to tackling similar challenges in the future.

3. **Use Positive Reinforcement**

   Remind your teen of their past successes and strengths.

   - *Purpose:* To cultivate a growth mindset in your teenager, where challenges are seen as opportunities for development.
   - *Why It's Important:* Positive reinforcement not only shifts the focus from failure to learning and growth, but it also plays a significant role in boosting your teen's self-esteem and confidence in their abilities.
   - *Outcome:* A more resilient and motivated attitude toward future challenges.

4. **Promote Independence and Self-Advocacy**

   Encourage your student to take independent actions.

   - *Purpose:* To build your teen's self-efficacy and self-advocacy.
   - *Why It's Important:* Fostering independence is crucial, as it not only prepares your almost-adult for real-world challenges and decision-making, but it also empowers them to take charge of their own learning and problem-solving.
   - *Outcome:* A self-reliant and proactive approach to learning and life's obstacles.

By following these steps, parents can guide their teenagers through setbacks, helping them build essential life skills.

Expanding Resilience: More Strategies for Parents

Let's delve deeper into strategies you can adopt to foster growth and resilience in your young adult.

1. **Creating a growth mindset environment.** You can encourage your teen to view setbacks as opportunities for learning rather than reflections of their abilities. This involves changing the language around failure and success. Praise effort and strategy over innate talent or intelligence. Emphasize the value of persistence and the learning process itself.

    Common setback example: Your 12th grader is struggling in a subject like math or science.

    - *Avoid:* Saying, "You're just not good at this subject," when your student struggles in a particular area like math is not helpful.
    - *Shift:* Instead, say, "Math can be challenging, but your effort can make a big difference. Let's see how we can tackle this together."
    - *The reason:* This shift moves away from labeling your teen's ability as fixed and inherent. It emphasizes the student's control over their learning process through effort and strategy. This encouragement to engage actively with challenging material fosters a growth mindset, where abilities are viewed as developable rather than static. It helps your teenager to approach difficulties with a more positive and proactive attitude, which is essential for learning and improvement.

2. **Effective communication techniques.** When discussing setbacks, use scripts and talking points that are constructive and supportive. This approach shifts the focus from blame to constructive improvement.

Common setback example: Your student receives a lower-than-expected grade on a major test or project.

- *Avoid:* Saying, "You failed because you didn't study hard enough" places blame.
- *Shift:* Try saying, "Let's look at how you prepared and see what we can do differently next time."
- *The reason:* This shift focuses on the process and effort rather than the outcome. Blaming language can demotivate and discourage your student, making them feel incapable or judged. By exploring how they prepared and discussing different strategies for the future, you encourage a problem-solving mindset. This approach fosters a sense of empowerment and responsibility. It helps them understand that setbacks are not failures but opportunities to learn and grow.

3. **Building support systems.** Encourage your student to seek support from peers, teachers, and family members. A strong support system provides a safe space for students to express their frustrations and fears and to seek advice and encouragement.

Common setback example: Your student has difficulty in understanding a complex topic or a project's requirements.

- *Avoid:* Insisting on solving every problem for them, like calling the teacher immediately to discuss a grade or project requirements, will not foster independence.
- *Shift:* Ask, "Have you thought about discussing your concerns with your teacher? They might offer some valuable insight."

- *The reason:* This shift encourages the development of self-advocacy and independence. By suggesting that your teen seek support from teachers and peers, you are helping them build important communication skills and learn to navigate challenges on their own. This approach also fosters a sense of responsibility and confidence, as your student realizes they can seek solutions and advocate for their needs. Furthermore, by using their support systems, your student gains diverse perspectives and advice, which can help in overcoming complex challenges.

4. **Developing problem-solving skills.** Teach your teen to analyze setbacks critically. Discuss what went wrong, why it might have happened, and how a different approach could lead to a better outcome.

   Common setback example: Receiving unexpected feedback or criticism on a major essay or project.

   - *Avoid:* Dismissing feedback or immediately defending your student's work without thorough analysis is not helpful.
   - *Shift:* Suggest, "Let's review the feedback together. What are the key points? How can we use this as a learning opportunity to improve?"
   - *The reason:* This shift helps your teen develop critical analysis and problem-solving skills. Rather than seeing feedback or criticism as purely negative, reviewing it together reframes it as a tool for learning and improvement. This process teaches your teenager to approach challenges with an open mind and a willingness to adapt and grow, which are invaluable skills in academics and life.

5. **Emotional intelligence development.** Help your teen understand and manage the emotions that come with setbacks. Discussing feelings of disappointment, frustration, or anxiety can help them develop emotional intelligence, which is key in handling challenges effectively.

   Common setback example: Feeling overwhelmed by the pressure of upcoming final exams or college application deadlines.

   - *Avoid:* Minimizing their stress or emotions by saying things like, "Just don't worry about it" or "It's not that big of a deal," is not helpful.
   - *Shift:* Instead, open a dialogue with, "It sounds like you're feeling really stressed about your exams. What's on your mind?" Encourage your teen to express their feelings, and then discuss strategies for managing stress and anxiety.
   - *The reason:* By acknowledging and discussing their emotions rather than dismissing them, you validate their feelings and demonstrate that it's okay to feel overwhelmed or anxious. This open dialogue creates a safe space for your teenager to explore and understand their emotions, which is a critical aspect of emotional intelligence. Developing emotional intelligence helps your teen become more self-aware, manage their emotions effectively, and communicate their feelings constructively. It equips them with the skills to handle emotional challenges in the future, leading to better decision-making, relationships, and overall mental health. Encouraging this open and understanding approach to emotions lays a strong foundation for them to navigate life's challenges with resilience and emotional agility.

Closing Advice

Critical self-reflection and problem-solving are not just for supporting your student through academic challenges, but also for preparing them for the broader, often unpredictable journey of life. It's about empowering them to face the world with poise and strength. Our role as parent isn't to shield our children from every hardship, but to equip them with the tools to navigate and grow from these experiences. By embracing setbacks as natural and beneficial, we support our high school seniors, paving their way to becoming resilient, confident young adults ready to take on the world.

Conversation Starters

- I noticed you seemed a bit down after your math test. Want to talk about what was tough in it?
- How do you feel about the feedback you got on your science project? Let's chat about it and see how you can use it to improve.
- I saw you've been having a hard time with history lately. What part of it is the most challenging for you?
- You seemed really disappointed after the game/practice. What happened, and how are you feeling about it?
- I've noticed you haven't been spending much time with [friend's name] recently. Is everything okay?
- It seems like forgetting your English assignment really bothered you. What can we do together to help you stay organized?
- You've been so busy with school and activities. Are you feeling overwhelmed? Let's talk about it.
- Have you thought about how you might talk to your teacher about the challenges you're facing in class?
- Balancing homework and your hobbies seems challenging. How do you think we could plan your week better?
- I know choosing a college course/college can be tough. What are your thoughts about it, and how can I help?

Chapter 7
OVERCOMING PROCRASTINATION

How to support your student in finding motivation

Leron McAdoo
Educational Consultant, Arkansas

Through lecturing in schools in and out of the country under my educational motivation brand, Mctivated, I've observed that student procrastination isn't an inherent default behavior. My 30-plus years as a classroom practitioner have allowed me to explore the challenge of student engagement. My experiences highlight the potential for overcoming procrastination. This behavior often results in hurried and incomplete assignments stemming from fear of failure, the pursuit of perfection, a lack of understanding, organizational issues, and low interest. However, fostering self-awareness in students can positively impact their motivation, enabling them to actively engage, produce quality work, and become "Mctivated" to reach the next level of academic excellence and self-development.

A Look at Procrastination

Student engagement has decreased significantly since COVID. One of the biggest indicators of that decline is the levels of procrastination I've witnessed. Procrastination had become an adopted trait and left teachers looking into the eyes of students who return the gaze with a lazy stare. Assignments are rushed, incomplete, or lifeless. Defined as the act of delaying or postponing an action, procrastination is a complex and real phenomenon rooted in various fears and challenges. Understanding these underlying factors is crucial in developing effective strategies to combat procrastination and empower students to navigate the academic landscape with confidence and resilience. Below are several strategies that I have used or seen working with students, as well as with my own children.

Addressing fear of failure

One significant cause of student procrastination is **the fear of failure**. The pressure to meet expectations, whether self-imposed or externally driven, can paralyze students, leading them to put off tasks in a desperate attempt to avoid potential disappointment. The looming specter of disapproval, be it from peers, teachers, or family, also contributes to this delay tactic. The desire to attain perfection becomes a double-edged sword, often hindering progress rather than fostering excellence. The idea of perfection can be a path to procrastination. An artist mentor of mine always said it's better to have 18 completed paintings than to have 18 attempts at a painting not brought to completion. Here are some ways to encourage progress:

- **Provide an open space.** Having an open space is different from having a safe space. An open space encourages your student to talk freely about their fears, as well as their hopes and joys. Teens should have an open space at home and school where they can discuss concerns without judgment.

- **Embrace the idea that progress is more important than perfection.** This allows your teen to navigate their academic and personal journeys with a healthier mindset. The pursuit of perfection can overwhelm students and hinder their ability to take risks and learn from mistakes. Progress is about growth and improvement.
- **Shift the focus from perfection to completion.** Finished work holds more value than unrealized aspirations. Remind your student that it's better to have work completed than to have a brilliant but unfinished attempt.
- **Encourage healthy coping skills.** This could include mindfulness techniques, time-management skills, or other stress-relief activities. These skills enhance your student's overall well-being by equipping them with valuable tools to manage stress.
- **Celebrate achievements and milestones.** Teens being praised for doing work helps reinforce that behavior, while also inspiring them to recognize that their own goals build confidence.

Addressing organization

Another factor contributing to student procrastination is **a lack of understanding or organization**. When faced with a complex task or an overwhelming amount of work, students may struggle to comprehend the requirements or fail to organize their thoughts effectively. Confusion and disarray create a breeding ground for procrastination, as students feel ill-equipped to tackle the challenge at hand. As an educator, I would much rather have an assignment turned in on time with an opportunity to make corrections than to have a late assignment.

- **Break it down.** When you break down assignments into smaller parts, it becomes more manageable. This approach alleviates the pressure associated with completing an entire project at once. Your teen will feel a sense of accomplishment at each step.

- **Take advantage of organizational tools.** Organizational tools such as checklists, timelines, or mind maps are helpful. Checklists ensure that no crucial step is overlooked, timelines offer a visual representation of deadlines, and mind maps help organize thoughts and ideas. By using these tools, your student can enhance their efficiency, stay organized, and better manage their academic responsibilities.

- **Work together.** Students should share drafts or preliminary work. This collaborative approach enables them to receive valuable feedback from peers or instructors, fostering a constructive learning environment. This process encourages open communication and contributes to a well-rounded and polished assignment.

- **Establish a routine.** A well-structured daily or weekly schedule can help your student prioritize tasks, allocate time efficiently, and create a sense of stability in their academic and personal lives. This routine not only aids in time management, but it also provides a framework for developing good study habits.

- **Create rapport with teachers.** Seniors can benefit from cultivating a respectful relationship with their teachers, providing an avenue for seeking clarifications, updates, or guidance. Teachers welcome questions and are more likely to be responsive to students who have established a connection with them.

Addressing student interest

Tasks that students find uninteresting pose a unique challenge. Low levels of concentration, energy, or confidence can derail even the most well-intentioned student, making it difficult to muster the motivation required to complete the assignment. The absence of intrinsic interest can be a formidable barrier, leading to a sense of apathy and detachment. Gone are the days when schools can simply place information in front of students and expect them to readily engage.

- **Learn to relate.** In certain assignments, your teen may need to generate interest by relating the task to their own perspective. When assignments become personally meaningful, they gain significance. This approach, when it can be used, not only facilitates a more captivating learning experience, but it also enables your student to identify ways to integrate their unique talents and gifts into the task at hand.
- **Collaborate.** Working with others fosters a dynamic exchange of ideas and perspectives, creating a more engaging and stimulating environment for everyone involved. This collaborative approach not only enhances the overall learning experience, but it also promotes a sense of camaraderie among individuals in the group.
- **Persevere.** Navigating an assignment that they don't have an interest in provides an opportunity to develop valuable skills, such as perseverance, discipline, and adaptability. These experiences contribute to a well-rounded education and offer a chance for personal growth and skill development.
- **Self-advocate.** Your student can ask for an alternative assignment. Your student should approach the teacher respectfully and clearly articulate what they would like to submit, being mindful of the original assignment's learning objectives.

Being grateful for the teacher's consideration and flexibility can make this a positive and constructive dialogue.

- **Develop intrinsic motivation.** By aligning school assignments with personal growth and skill development, your teen can uncover intrinsic motivation. Whether striving for specific grades, acknowledging progress, or seeking recognition for achievements, academic goals serve as powerful motivators, even when the tasks themselves may not be inherently interesting. This connection between personal development and academic success reinforces a sense of purpose, driving your student to engage actively in their schoolwork.

Addressing feeling overwhelmed

The emotional toll of procrastination is evident in the **feelings of anxiety, distraction,** and **overwhelm** that students often experience. As deadlines approach and work piles up, the weight of uncompleted tasks becomes increasingly burdensome. This cascade of negative emotions further exacerbates the cycle of procrastination, creating a self-fulfilling prophecy where students find themselves perpetually falling behind. It's heartbreaking to see students at the end of the year, especially seniors, attempting to make up a semester's worth of work in two weeks—but it always happens. And there are even those who don't manage to make it to graduation.

- **Teach self-awareness.** Teaching teens self-awareness gives them a valuable tool for managing stress and navigating challenges. It equips students with the ability to recognize their emotions, strengths, and areas for improvement, fostering resilience and emotional intelligence. This approach empowers students to move forward with a greater sense of self-control and confidence.

- **Be lenient.** Helping students be lenient with themselves when they are stressed allows them to keep everything in perspective. Self-compassion helps students learn to acknowledge their efforts and progress, even when facing challenging tasks. Encouraging a mindset of self-forgiveness and understanding fosters resilience and promotes a healthier approach to academic and personal challenges.
- **Identify obstacles.** Identifying obstacles in their learning journey empowers teens to navigate challenges more effectively. With this skill, they can proactively address difficulties and seek appropriate support or strategies to overcome them.
- **Check in regularly.** Teach teens the practice of regular check-ins. This involves regularly assessing their progress. There is a tendency for people to withdraw from others when they face difficulty. By implementing regular check-ins, students can maintain a connection and a sense of control over their workload.
- **Choose an accountability partner.** Introduce the concept of having an accountability partner. Encouraging your teen to seek a friend, family member, or mentor as an accountability partner can offer valuable motivation and support. This collaborative approach fosters a sense of responsibility and also creates a supportive network for students as they encounter academic challenges.

A Look at Motivation

As a motivational speaker, career and college coach, and educational consultant, I have seen motivation work to ignite students and staff. With strategic approaches and a shift in mindset, it is possible to transform student procrastination with motivation.

All the fears, all the lack of skills, and all the lack of interest that cause procrastination can be addressed with a change in perspective. I always say, "An attitude change is an everything change." Students must search inside themselves to identify the root cause of procrastination, whether it's fear of failure, disapproval, or the pursuit of perfection. Recognizing the underlying issue is the first step toward addressing and overcoming it. Procrastination may be widespread, but it is a personal struggle.

Too many times students think the task before them is going to be easy, quickly done, or accomplished without preparation. And, at times, motivation can make them feel as though they are ready—until they encounter an obstacle. The true purpose of motivation is to help you become more self-aware. By recognizing the specific situations or tasks that evoke avoidance behavior, you can develop targeted strategies to address these challenges head-on. Moreover, self-awareness enables individuals to identify negative self-talk and replace it with more constructive and motivating internal dialogue. This heightened self-awareness fosters a **proactive mindset**, empowering individuals to confront obstacles, set realistic goals, and cultivate a sense of accountability, steering them away from the clutches of procrastination.

Cultivating a growth mindset is fundamental in shifting from procrastination to motivation. Embracing challenges as opportunities to learn and viewing failures as stepping stones toward improvement fosters resilience and determination. By guiding your student to reframe setbacks as part of the learning process, you can help your student develop a more positive and proactive approach to their studies. Self-reflection, realistic goal setting, organization, intrinsic motivation, and a growth mindset are ways to break free from the chains of procrastination and embark on a path of academic success fueled by genuine motivation and enthusiasm.

Closing Advice

I know that student procrastination can be conquered. Drawing on more than 30 years as an educator, I've delved into the challenge of student engagement, highlighting the potential for overcoming procrastination. It is self-awareness in students that can positively influence their motivation, allowing them to actively participate, produce high-quality work, and become "Mctivated" to achieve higher levels academically and personally.

Chapter 8
NAVIGATING STUDENT-TEACHER RELATIONSHIPS

How to help your senior build
rapport with educators

Amybeth Taylor
High School English Teacher, New Hampshire

Senior year is a thrilling yet daunting time. As parents, we share our children's emotions and strive to assist them with future planning, while also striving to maintain a balance between guidance and interference. Your teenager appreciates your interest and concern, though their desire for your involvement can vary greatly from one individual to another. I proofread dozens of college essays each year, and it is heartwarming to read how many of my students credit a parent or other trusted adult for their influence and support.

When my son was applying to colleges, I was eager to help with everything, from his application essay to obtaining letters of recommendation from teachers. I wanted to be involved, and I wanted everything to go smoothly for him. However, he wanted to take charge of the process and asked me to step back. Despite feeling a bit hurt, I respected his wishes and waited for him to ask for help, because professionally I know that—whether heading to college or pursuing other paths—it's crucial for a student's voice and personality to shine through their planning. Too much parental involvement can overshadow this, which is counterproductive. College admissions representatives value authenticity.

As a high school English teacher who works with 11th and 12th graders, I get to enjoy the process of college and future planning with students from a safe distance; I understand the boundary between solicited and unsolicited advice. Most students are capable of asking teachers, counselors, and parents for help as needed, whether it's help with filling out college applications or with letters of recommendation. Occasionally I work with students whose parents have enlisted the help of a private college counselor to help mediate and facilitate the college application process. Trust your instincts, assess how involved you want to be, and ask your child how you can be of assistance.

How Can Students Build Relationships with Teachers if They Haven't Already?

Some students enter senior year with a clear understanding of where they stand with at least one teacher, and they feel comfortable approaching that teacher for a reference or letter of recommendation. Many other students experience anxiety and hesitation, feeling daunted about having to ask teachers for recommendations. Often, this is because they don't feel as if they have built a strong enough relationship with teachers who can write about their personal and academic strengths.

To build rapport, help your senior consider:

- It's never too late to put in the effort to build relationships with trusted teachers, counselors, or advisers.
- Don't be afraid of small talk. If you want your teachers to get to know you, spend some time getting to know them also. A good way to start is by simply asking, "How is your day going?"
- Respect the teacher and the class by putting in effort, doing the work, participating in class discussions, and asking questions to demonstrate interest.
- Consider communicating with a teacher after class. Taking a few minutes to ask questions or add follow-up commentary on the class's content is a perfect way to show interest and build a connection.
- Join a club that a respected teacher advises. That way, the teacher gets a chance to see you outside of the classroom setting.
- Just going out of your way to have a normal conversation with your teacher or counselor is a good way to build an initial connection, which makes subsequent conversations less nerve-racking and more natural, making it easier to build a relationship.

Don't let your student underestimate the relationships they have already established with teachers. While your student may not feel close to a teacher, their presence, hard work, and respect toward teachers and classmates creates a positive impression. Teachers recognize that. Trust that your student has already established relationships with past and present teachers.

A Privilege and a Professional Obligation

At the start of the year, I remind students that teachers are privileged to help with college applications and future planning. It is also part of a teacher's job to write letters of recommendation and fill out the reference questionnaires many colleges and employers require. Teachers feel honored when a student respects them enough to request a recommendation.

Students should generally ask for letters from two teachers. Who they ask depends on their intended major and where they are applying. Some colleges and programs will specify who those letters should be from, many preferring one from a math or science teacher and a second from an English teacher. If a student is applying to a fine arts program, they will need a letter from an art or music teacher in addition to their portfolio or audition requirement. The school counselor writes a separate letter, which is fairly standard for most, if not all, colleges applied to through Common App. When all is said and done, students will submit two to three letters of recommendation. For students who are able to include an additional letter, they may have the chance to also ask a coach or club adviser. The Family Educational Rights and Privacy Act waives a student's right to see those recommendations, so it's best to ask those individuals who a student knows will represent them strongly. Students should consider asking for recommendation letters from teachers who:

- Know them from multiple classes and experiences
- Teach classes related to their intended college major or career
- Taught classes where they performed exceptionally well
- Taught classes they enjoyed and excelled in
- Know them well, both personally and academically

Here are some other considerations in asking for a recommendation letter:

- Ask for recommendations in August or September when teachers are feeling recharged.
- Ask teachers in person for a letter of recommendation whenever possible.
- Compose a professional-sounding email with your request if you are unable to ask teachers in person for some reason.
- Allow plenty of time between when you ask for a recommendation and when your earliest application is due.
- Give teachers a copy of your résumé or a "brag sheet."
- Be prepared for the possibility that teachers and counselors may want to chat with you in person for a few minutes to get a better idea about your future plans so they know what to include in your recommendation.
- Gently remind teachers of the deadline if it's near and a letter is still pending, and thank them for their time.

In-Person Script: "Hi, Mr. or Ms. ___, I am wondering if you would be willing to write a recommendation letter on my behalf? I am applying to ___ with a deadline of ___ . Here is a copy of my résumé. Please let me know if there is anything else I can share with you that would be helpful. Thank you. I really appreciate it."

Email Script: Dear Mr. or Ms. ___, I am wondering if you would be willing to write a recommendation letter on my behalf. I am applying to ___ with a deadline of ___ . I am attaching a copy of my résumé to this email. Please let me know if there is anything else I can share with you that would be helpful. I appreciate your time and help. Thank you, ___

VERY IMPORTANT: Don't forget to follow up with a thank you! So many students forget this most important step. Remember that your teachers and counselor have taken the time to compose a thoughtful recommendation on your behalf. It is so important to acknowledge that you are grateful for their help and appreciative of their time. (Educators keep and cherish those thank you notes forever.)

What is the Role of the School Counselor and Faculty Adviser?

The school counselor can be an amazing resource and guide as students plan for life after high school. Whether an individual's plan involves college, trade school, or immediate employment, a school counselor is there to help.

Most counselors will schedule student meetings in the spring of junior year or early in senior year to gauge where a student is in their planning and to help them set deadlines for the college application process. If your student does not hear from their counselor, encourage them to set up a meeting. It is absolutely okay for parents to help out if a student does not feel comfortable taking the initiative. In fact, it is better to act early than to wait until important deadlines have passed. Communicate via email first, and if you do not get a reply within a couple of days, follow up with a polite phone call.

An effective email might read: Dear ____ , My student, ____ , a current 12th grader, is hoping to complete their earliest college applications by ____ . They respect your guidance and would appreciate a planning meeting at your earliest convenience. As this is our first time navigating this process, we may have questions. Is email the best way to communicate with you? Thank you for all you do. Best, ____ [your contact information]

Some questions to ask your student's counselor may include:

- Has my student already created a Common App account?
- Will there be a financial aid information night when parents and students will hear about the FAFSA, scholarship opportunities, and other ways to finance college?
- Is there a free resource available to parents and students to help with the college admissions process and financial aid?
- If my student is applying early action or early decision, when will they be meeting with you in September to make sure they have all of their application materials ready?
- Can you help my student decide which school to apply to early decision as opposed to early action and regular decision? (A student can only apply to one school early decision, because it is a binding agreement if accepted.)

Involving the faculty adviser

If students and parents have concerns along the way, or if additional help is needed, most schools now have an advisory program. Students are assigned a faculty adviser when they begin 9th grade and, ideally, the adviser will work with a student for all four years of high school. It is the adviser's role to not only guide students through their high school experience, but also to sometimes be a liaison between home and school. If your student needs assistance setting up appointments with the school counselor or asking teachers for recommendations, the adviser is an excellent resource.

Students may ask their adviser for help with:

- Deciding who to ask for a recommendation letter
- Following up on a pending letter of recommendation from a teacher

- Completing parts of the college application or finding someone who can help
- Writing a recommendation letter, given their familiarity with the student

If your student doesn't have a faculty adviser, they should ask their counselor for this support.

The College Essay

See if your student's school offers a college essay writing workshop the summer prior to 12th grade. Some schools offer such workshops free or can connect families with resources for assistance. Early discussion and planning will help to eliminate some of the stress that accompanies the busy fall months of senior year. If a student's 11th- or 12th-grade English teacher does not include college application essays as part of the curriculum, your student may appreciate help with writing and editing application and supplemental essays.

Here are some helpful guidelines:

- Ask the counseling office if an essay-writing workshop will be offered at the school during the summer or if they know of a workshop available elsewhere.
- Consider one of the many online college essay-writing workshops. While some charge a fee, there are plenty of free resources available online.
- A student can ask their English teacher or guidance counselor if they are willing to help with editing and proofreading.
- While parents can be helpful sounding boards, be careful that your voice does not begin to dominate the essay. I counsel students to seek advice from one or two individuals

- Check the requirements for each college application. Is a supplemental essay required, such as a "Why Us" statement? If a college requires more than one writing sample, allow plenty of time by planning ahead.

- Plan on multiple drafts. Students who I have worked with in the past on college essays are amazed at what unfolds in their writing when they are willing to see it transform through multiple drafts.

The essay is an important part of the college application. An admissions rep will be reading it—along with hundreds of other essays.

Challenges Faced by Students with Unconventional Paths

I wrote a recommendation letter recently for a student who approached me at the last minute because he was unsure about who to ask. He moved around, switched high schools several times, and landed in my 11th-grade English class. He was a quieter student, faced with the challenges of having to navigate a new town, new school, and new friends. January of his senior year rolled around, and he still didn't have a teacher letter of recommendation. When he approached me, I could tell that he was nervous about asking. I remember this individual as a respectful, hardworking student, so I was happy to write a letter on his behalf. It does not take long for teachers to assess students academically and personally in order to provide a glowing recommendation.

Homeschooled students may feel stressed about college applications. They should seek out opportunities to get involved in school or recreational sports teams or other community-organized activities. Any coach, club adviser, or employer can provide recommendations.

Closing Advice

We want to strike a balance between help and interference. My college sophomore still calls me for advice and help when needed, but I have to respect the fact that he needs space to become who he wants to be. As I now begin the college process again with my middle child, I find that I have to resist the urge to offer what she might consider interference. Some of the ways in which I will try to help, however, are in establishing a timeline for college applications, helping with research on different colleges, and discussing financial options. I know that I have to be an emotional support as much as a source of information. It's not just about the practical steps, but also about understanding and empathy.

We recently visited a highly competitive college and met the most impressive student tour guide. What made this student so impressive was not only his depth of knowledge about the school, but also his reminder that the right path will work itself out for each individual. During this emotional time for parents and their college-bound children, that is one of the best pieces of advice I can imagine getting or giving. The right path will work itself out for each individual.

Conversation Starters

- What are your feelings about senior year and post-graduation plans?
- Which colleges do you plan to apply to?
- Have you created a list or spreadsheet of colleges, application requirements, deadlines, and costs that you can share with me?
- Do you know where to search for scholarships?
- Which teachers will you ask for recommendation letters?
- Do you have a résumé or want help creating one?
- What's your comfort level with asking for help from your adviser or counselor?

Chapter 9
PLANNING THE POSTSECONDARY ROUTE

How your student's high school
helps with the process

Courtney Walker
2024 GASSP Georgia Assistant Principal of the Year

"Sen·ior·i·tis" is defined by Great Hearts Academies as "a supposed affliction of students in their final year of high school or college, characterized by a decline in motivation or performance."

Many seniors find themselves battling apathy and a lack of motivation to give it one last hoorah before they don that cap and gown (read more on the Senior Slump in Chapter 11). However, others spring into gear and overload their plates in hopes that a last-ditch effort can change their trajectory into adulthood. Regardless of which category your 12th grader falls into, they can't take on this last year of school alone. Dismantling some of the myths or misconceptions of 12th grade can help you navigate this last year of high school.

Parent Misconceptions

Raise your hand if you've believed any of the myths below:

- "My daughter isn't sure what she wants to pursue. She can figure that out after she graduates."
- "My senior has to go to college to be successful."
- "My student's teachers will reach out if there are problems."
- "My student's counselor will help them get into college or find a job."

It's okay. These misconceptions have fooled the very best, most engaged parents. It's important to understand, though, why believing these myths can negatively impact your teen's future and what you can do to get ahead of the false narrative.

While teachers, school counselors, and administrators are devoted to ensuring seniors cross the finish line and earn their high school diplomas, relying solely on educators' expertise to guide your child's postsecondary plans can be a mistake. Your senior needs *you* to support their interests, passions, abilities, and plans after graduation.

To offer optimal support for your student, it is important first to consider what's happening inside the brain of a 12th grader and what pressures or decisions they are facing. This might be the most important year yet, because your influence and guidance can help chart the course for your student's first steps into the adult world.

Cognitive Development and Decision-Making

Teenagers' brains and how they make decisions are not like that of an adult. Their actions are "guided more by the emotional and reactive amygdala and less by the thoughtful, logical frontal cortex," according to the American Academy of Child & Adolescent Psychiatry, meaning they cannot reason through major decisions using logic. Their decisions are impulsive and reactive to their current circumstances. A 12th-grade student needs you to provide reason and caution when approaching life-changing decisions, such as whether or not to attend college, make major financial commitments such as loans, or select a safe living environment after moving out of your home.

According to Stanford Medicine, "The rational part of a teen's brain isn't fully developed and won't be until age 25 or so....In teens' brains, the connections between the emotional part of the brain and the decision-making center are still developing—and not always at the same rate. That's why when teens have overwhelming emotional input, they can't explain later what they were thinking." Their feelings often outweigh their reasoning.

If you want to bring up the conversation about their postsecondary plans, don't haphazardly toss the subject out to your teenager when they are emotional. You will likely get an irrational response. Instead, consider taking them out for a fun dinner when you have time to help them sift through the pressures in the planning process so that they are more responsive to logical, thoughtful decision-making.

Pressures in the Planning

It's easy to assume that your high school student should be carefree and full of excitement about the next phase of life. However, the opposite is often true. Students entering 12th grade can be anxious and overwhelmed with many internal and external pressures surrounding their postsecondary plans, including pleasing their parents, overloading themselves to "beef up" applications, comparing themselves to their friends' successes, paying for it all, and wrestling with the dreaded question, "What if I don't...?"

First, whether you feel like you and your teen are the best of friends or you're enemies stepping into lines of battle, your student is still concerned with pleasing you. All children, whether they are 8 or 18, seek the approval and love of their parents. They may not agree with your opinions or stance, especially concerning their first steps as an adult, but they most certainly do not want you to feel disappointed in them. Give them some space to figure things out and offer grace if it takes a few rounds to land on a plan that's comfortable for you both.

Overscheduling

We often think that senior year is the time to load a student's plate with the most rigorous classes, additional extracurricular activities, or numerous leadership roles. After all, that's the only way they will get into the best colleges, right? Unfortunately, it can be a recipe for disaster. At this point, let their body of work speak for itself. Throwing "extras" onto their plates won't better secure their enrollment; it will send them into a spiral. If your student was able to balance honors classes and multiple extracurricular activities throughout high school, that's fantastic! Spend time helping them craft their experiences into a résumé to share with their counselor, teachers, or coaches for letters of recommendation. Consider their current involvement and help them set goals, such as looking for a single community service project through their club or expanding on a class project they've already completed to use as tutoring materials for younger students. It's quality, not quantity.

Peer pressure

Your senior is going to feel some pressure directly connected to their peers. They are listening as the boy next to them in class announces he was accepted into his tenth college. Your daughter's best friend boasts with excitement that she just landed a summer internship out of state. Meanwhile, your daughter is terrified about moving 10 minutes down the road. It is normal for 12th graders to compare their postsecondary plans. However, they need you to reassure them that they can and will develop lots of new relationships during the next few years. Explain to them that you will work together, with the help of school personnel, to develop a plan that is just right for them. Breathe confidence in them and encourage them to be excited for their own journey.

Financial pressure

Even if your senior has a full academic scholarship to a major college or university, there will always be a little uncertainty about how they will pay for their expenses on their own. Many students have completed courses in financial literacy or personal finance, but many 12th graders aren't certain of how they will secure the funding for housing, tuition, or daily living expenses. Most high schools now have some type of graduation coach or college and career specialist on staff. Schedule a meeting with them and develop a financial plan as a family that will put your and your student's minds at ease.

Fear of failing

Fear of failure is looming. This stressor is often the heaviest. Students can become paralyzed with fear, imagining not being admitted to their dream school, not finding a job they love, or enrolling in the armed forces only to find it's too much. Those feelings of self-doubt can impact their academic performance and even mental health. Working together to develop a comfortable backup plan can help reduce stress.

Regardless of what pressures they are feeling, there are some major decisions and steps to consider in helping your senior prepare for life after graduation.

Key Processes and Help in Postsecondary Planning

It is important to meet with your child's school counselor between spring and summer of junior year. A senior's schedule is vital to ensuring they meet all graduation requirements and maximize the options available to them. Upperclassmen are usually provided with more options for classes, including additional advanced coursework, internship opportunities, or work-based learning courses. Oftentimes, schools will send home or publish a senior handbook or newsletter with a senior's schedule that includes important dates, details about special events, or critical resources for your child's success. These may also be listed on the school website.

Applications and letters of recommendation

Whether your child is planning to enroll in college or heading straight into the workforce, they will need letters of recommendation to accompany their applications. While a school counselor is prepared and willing to write a letter of recommendation, it can sometimes be more beneficial if a teacher, coach, or close family friend writes the letter. Whoever can best speak to the character, work ethic, and accomplishments of your senior is the best person for the job. Providing that person with a list of activities, accomplishments, and academic coursework can better prepare them to highlight your student's successes.

Financial aid and scholarships

This one can be scary. However, do not fear. Your child's school is there to help you find the many opportunities for pursuing scholarship possibilities. Many districts have established education foundations that provide financial assistance to students and are accessible by submitting essays, transcripts, and letters of recommendation. There are also major companies, such as College Board, that offer scholarships to students simply for using their websites or applications. Many students earn thousands of dollars for college because the guidance department helps connect them with the right resources or organizations.

The role of the teacher

Teachers can offer great support to your senior in the postsecondary planning process. From writing letters of recommendation to providing feedback on learning processes and preferences, teachers can help students tap into their natural abilities or talents. You know your 12th grader's passions, interests, and future plans. By working together, you can help your student identify career fields, areas of interest, and a possible major of study at a university or college. If your student has any type of disability or needs additional support through an individualized education plan or 504, a teacher can provide input about interventions or accommodations that might be considered in a college setting.

The role of the counselor

Like teachers, counselors support students in planning for life after high school. They work to support students in completing college applications, applying for financial aid or identifying scholarship opportunities, and even finding internships that align with their future career goals. Counselors also serve as a liaison between students, parents, teachers, and administrators. They can help connect families with community resources, such as clothing, food, and necessities, as well as extracurricular activities that support the development of your student.

The role of administrators

There are often many award and recognition opportunities for seniors, and these are typically chosen or decided by the school administration. If there are certain areas or skills in which your student excels and has shown significant involvement, reach out and ask if there are award and recognition possibilities that would highlight the accomplishments of your child. Administrators want to celebrate the successes of student leaders in their schools. If they are familiar with your student and are aware of their talents and gifts, they can often recommend them for additional awards and recognitions that will support their applications to college or a job.

Parent Dos and Don'ts

1. **Don't let your senior wait until they get out in the real world to decide what interests them.**

   Instead, reach out to your student's counselor and request any results from aptitude and/or interest surveys that were conducted at school. If there is not a survey on file, research some reputable surveys on the internet, have your student complete a few, and go over the results together.

2. **Don't force your expectations and passions on your senior.**

   Instead, listen. Your student is on the brink of adulthood. While they need help processing and reasoning through their decisions, your role is to encourage. They have their own passions, interests, and plans. Help them develop a plan to graduate enrolled, enlisted, or employed, and engaged as a leader in their community.

   • If college is the right fit, plan two visits during the spring before the start of 12th grade, one to a smaller, local school and one to a larger university farther away. This will help your senior narrow down the type of experience they want after graduation.

- If your senior wants to pursue a career right after high school, that requires a technical certification or real-world experience. Visit a technical institution or ask the school's work-based learning coordinator to look for a community-based internship that can prepare your student for their chosen career field.
- If your senior is interested in the military, ask the counselor to set up a meeting with a recruiter where you and your senior can ask questions and make an informed decision about whether the armed forces is the way to go.

3. **Don't skip the school's information nights or parent events.**

Instead, make it a celebration. Plan for time together after the event when you can sit down and discuss how you will work together to elicit help from school personnel in preparing for graduation. The school will often release updated information or key details about what major processes need to be completed in the coming months. Check the school website often for new information, and reach out to ask if any parent nights are scheduled.

4. **Don't allow your senior to be content with the comfortable.**

Instead, encourage your student to challenge themself. Becoming an adult comes with new experiences that are exciting but also a little intimidating. You don't want your teen to wake up years later feeling regret that they didn't take advantage of some key experiences that could have positively shaped their future (even if they seemed overwhelming at the time).

Reassure them that they can overcome any challenge, and remind them you will help when needed.

5. **Don't let the pace and excitement of senior year pass you by.**

    Instead, soak up these moments. Time slips by so quickly, and you will never get this year back. Enjoy the push and pull of your teen's indecisiveness and fight for independence. Support their desire to be treated like an adult, but step in when you see them struggling to find the best fit and feel for what's next.

Closing Advice

Your teen needs support in using reason and logic to make sound decisions concerning their postsecondary plans. You can help them decide whether they should pursue enrolling in college, enlisting in the military, or seeking employment. Partner with your teen's school for support in securing letters of recommendation, completing college applications, and creating a financial plan to support their next steps. While you may believe high school graduation wraps up the end of your parenting journey, you are only just beginning. Parenting adults is just as important.

Conversation Starters

- Do you think your school schedule is well set up for senior year? What are some classes or commitments that concern you?

- Have you thought about two educators who you can ask for letters of recommendation? Who are they and why did you choose them?

- Are you interested in attending college? If so, would you like to attend classes on a large or small campus? How far would you like to live from home?

- Are there any internships you would be interested in pursuing this year? When can we set up a meeting with your counselor to discuss those?

- What accomplishments are you most proud of? Are there some projects or service opportunities you can expand on this year?

Chapter 10
ONLINE PRESENCE

How to help your student own their online narrative

Timothy M. Dove
2011 and 2012 Ohio State Teacher of the Year

The beginning of a high schooler's senior year can be both exciting and frightening. It is a year of celebration and "lasts." For the reflective student, every event they participate in will be the last one they experience while in high school. This can be both celebratory and depressing. There is also a societal message of "the best years of your life are in high school." It is time to take advantage of skills and experience while planning for post-high school. The "What's next?" will continue to be a consideration this year. While the celebrations and struggles have been the focus of your senior's life for the last few years, the possibilities of the future should be exciting!

Social media and online life have been a part of your high school student's life since they can remember. They have never known a time without personal phones, tablets, and other electronic devices with access to the internet. Even as I write this, I know that referencing certain devices, programs, and apps will be dated in just a few years. As an example, references to Myspace, CompuServe, Ask Jeeves, and AOL either bring a chuckle or confusion. These were the initial giants of the online landscape. This chapter will not be a history lesson, however; the point is to look at the universal issues around social media, access, and how people are perceived and use the internet to access information about each other.

If you have read the *11th Grade Ready* book of this series, use this chapter as a reminder of the importance of and strategies for creating a more focused use of social media. If you feel like you don't need a refresher, you can skip to page 104, "The Importance of Following," near the end of this chapter.

High schoolers are digital natives and know a great deal about the electronic landscape in which they grew up, but do not confuse that with knowing everything about how it is used by others and appreciating the possible unintended consequences of their online activities. Search techniques, the use of AI, the development of basic programs/bots, and understanding the use of powerful algorithms are usually not fully appreciated even by 12th grade. I have even been surprised by how many seniors do not understand or know how to protect their personal data and location. Access as a convenience is great, but it can also be a small step toward becoming "creepy" as, for example, when you are in a brick-and-mortar store and your phone alerts you to a possible sale in the place you just left as you head for the parking lot.

Why an Online Presence Needs a Review

During my work with high school juniors and seniors, I taught a formal set of lessons to help students redefine their web presence. All of us have a web presence. It has been determined through our own efforts, but also by many others, including friends, family, schools, coworkers, and even strangers. Whether we posted the content or someone else did, tagging us, what was "cute," "funny," or "interesting" 10 years ago may no longer be so. Yet this information will always have a footprint on the internet.

There are times in our lives when we can make a new start. Your student's senior year should be one of them, if they haven't moved in this direction already. As your senior heads toward completing high school, it is time for them to become intentional and strategic in creating a professional adult presence on the web.

When reflecting on what your student would want as a web narrative, they need to consider the breadth of the audience. What age/generation is reviewing this web content? For what purpose would the content be reviewed? You can play a role in feedback and review. Often the people who are looking to fill a position for employment or learning opportunities are your age or older. Your point of view is valuable. Other adults in the student's life with expertise, experience, or knowledge can also be helpful in this conversation.

I suggest some things to consider before your student begins this process. Remember those who review your student's online presence can be the very people making decisions about their future learning opportunities, employment, and professional connection years from now. Your student should be able to review and have access to edit their online presence as time passes. Although anyone with tech savvy can find previous posts, pictures, and information, your student ultimately wants an avenue to push online traffic to an updated image as an adult. A LinkedIn URL is one example of a place to showcase a student's important experiences, skills, and knowledge that can be shared with others.

Some questions to ask your student:

- When was the last time you did a search for your name on the internet? What showed up?
- Are you happy with your current web presence (your own social media accounts and what shows up with searches of your name)?
- Do you have ideas about how your web presence could positively or negatively affect others' perceptions of you (for employment, internships, college, military applications)?
- What do you need to create and/or collect to present yourself online in the best way possible?

You can also share with your teen the missteps you may have made with your online presence in this process (we all have!).

Helping Your Student Take Control of Their Narrative

You've probably said, "I'm so glad social media was not a thing when I was growing up! I wouldn't want my life chronicled in such detail and available to anyone." So don't let that stop them! Here are six steps to cultivating a grown-up web presence:

Step 1. Select a professional name.

A good place to start to reinvent one's web presence is to decide on a professional, formal name you will be known as moving forward. Some nicknames may not be helpful in how others perceive you. For instance, your soon-to-be adult might want to use their given name, Michael, instead of Mikey.

Step 2. Use email as a way to connect.

An email account is the most basic way to communicate on the web and needs to reflect your identity as an adult moving forward. Avoid an email that is "cute," seen as inappropriate, or from when you were eight years old and doesn't make sense anymore. Go to an email provider (such as Google or Yahoo) and create a new account, which should be:

- Easy to remember
- A brief address and connected to your professional adult name

As an example, my email address is TMDedc@gmail.com (my initials and "edc" for Education Concepts, my consulting group). Because many Gmail account names are already established, Google will make a suggestion based on what you requested and usually add a series of numbers. Don't just accept the first suggestion; play around with options that make sense. You may find something that you really like. "TDoveEd@gmail.com" will be perceived much differently than "HappyDad#1@gmail.com" or "PartyAnimal12@gmail.com." Due to its brevity, my chosen address can also be typed quickly and has less chance of being typed incorrectly. You can imagine the opportunities for error with an email address such as "ILovetoTeachmostoftheTime5321@gmail.com."

Step 3. Find a space to post and share for new and existing contacts.

You should have a place to send traffic after you reset and control your personal narrative. LinkedIn is one such space. It is fairly simple to set up, inexpensive (free for the basic level), and gives the individual an opportunity to network with others in similar or supportive fields. According to its current usage agreement, the platform can be used by those 16 and older.

Not all social media is the same. Do not treat LinkedIn as Facebook or Instagram for the corporate world. As an example, the number of contacts you have through LinkedIn does not necessarily equate to "the more the better." The focus is not on collecting "likes," but on making helpful contacts. Although students are quick to point out that this platform and others are "dated" or "for old people," they are used by the very people they will need and want to connect with as they move beyond high school.

Step 4. Select a headshot that represents yourself well.

You would not go to a college scholarship interview or an important internship/job interview in cutoff shorts. You should present yourself in the online realm as a professional as well. Your photograph could be a formal head-and-shoulders picture or you with an icon in the background, but *you* need to be the focus of the picture. No group shots and *no* logos. This will avoid copyright issues, assumptions about you, or the awkwardness that comes from wearing an Ohio State sweatshirt while applying to the University of Michigan for admission or employment.

Step 5. Write a few sentences about yourself.

If you were going to introduce your professional self, what would you share? Use these as possible prompts: What holds your current interest/passion? Explain briefly why and/or what feeds this interest and/or passion. Consider your audience and be honest. This will be a prominent part of the LinkedIn profile page.

Step 6. Get a start!

To create a LinkedIn account, go to linkedin.com/uas/login.

The website is user-friendly and walks you through the fields. A few things to keep in mind:

- Do not make up any information.
- For education, include your high school name and location and any interests (i.e., favorite classes and extracurriculars) in the "groups" section with a short narrative.
- For employment, share any current part-time job or other experiences as an intern, coach, counselor, etc. Give your current job and focus as "Student."

If your student has privacy issues or concerns, invite them to discuss their thoughts with you or another engaged adult, like a teacher or adviser. As a prompt for a conversation you might ask, "How do you share information to invite conversation with new professional contacts without 'oversharing?' What might oversharing include?"

Once the LinkedIn account is set up, an example of what the *final* URL should look like is something such as linkedin.com/in/tmdove. Remember that when the account is set up, it is possible to modify what the company gave as an initial URL to something a bit shorter and connected to your student's name.

Conversation Starters (and Answers!)

The following are conversation starters to share *after* your student has had time to think through a revamp of their web presence. The bullet points below the questions are responses from my junior and senior students as they went through the process.

1. Is your LinkedIn page complete? What else might you change later and why?
    - "As the school year goes on, and even beyond that as my careers as a student and employee continue, I can certainly add information as I gain it in areas such as volunteer work, organizations I have been associated with, and my employment status."

- "I may change my interests/short biography as my interests vary over time."

2. Who are your potential audiences for this page about you?

    - "Future employers, admissions officers, and professional contacts are all potential audiences for this page."

3. What was frustrating about this experience (give any details)?

    - "As a student, I feel I don't have as much validity in each of my accomplishments or skills as I may not have developed them adequately enough to be important in the eyes of professional adults who could be viewing my page."
    - "I am not good with technology; therefore, this was a little bit of a hassle."

4. When did you experience being victorious (give any details)?

    - "When I remembered my involvement with clubs such as drama and French, it gave me a sense of hope for my validity. I have spent so much time in these two groups that, despite their general purpose not exactly being professional in itself, my time and experience within these groups has developed into life-altering lessons that I feel are substantial enough to have an impact on my professional life."
    - "I experienced this when I saw other contacts I could potentially reach out to on LinkedIn."

5. Describe something you did that you believe to be effective in presenting yourself in a positive way online.

    - "By giving a brief synopsis of my involvement in my employment, organizations, etc., I feel that I gave another nudge to anyone viewing my page into finding me a credible person."

- "I have a sophisticated and mature biography with an appropriate email to reach out to others."

6. How might this online work affect your future? Think about how this might relate to what is already there.

   - "As this is discovered by organizations in the future, the early growth of this page will allow it to transform and grow and, finally, mature much quicker than my peers who will not have the deep roots in this medium."
   - "This online work can show my progress and efforts as people message me/I message others to ask about any issues surrounding my future work."

7. What is some advice you would give to classmates/friends about this exercise?

   - "I would suggest spending perhaps an hour before beginning this page to do a self-reflection and come up with a solid list of groups you are involved in and some skills you not only gained from those positions, but also from life."
   - "I would suggest to my friends to start on this early in the year and continue to add to it and build a strong profile."

8. What did you learn about yourself in the process of creating a new online presence?

   - "I realized what my passions were and how I could use them to better the world."
   - "I learned that, from a strictly statistical standpoint, I am quite closer to an average student than to an overachiever."

- "I learned that there are so many different people online with different skill sets. This will help when I am trying to make connections."

- "I learned that I could do more to build my experiences and that this year will help me pursue my goals and actually create a positive influence in my community."

The Importance of Following

In moving toward "What's next?" your student might consider leveraging the advantages of social media connections. On many platforms, the user can invite and/or follow others. This includes groups. Following groups can help you gain current information and make yourself known. These "groups" can be colleges, programs, businesses, and/or military groups, in addition to individuals. Consider who you follow and/or friend and why—and share that with your senior. Their future direction and interests should help identify prospective groups. Remind your student to use their updated email or other accounts to move interested parties to their new online narrative. Once this process is started, make sure they visit their new email address and other platform sites they have created. It won't be helpful for someone to reach out if there is no timely response.

Here are a few more questions to get your student started and in the habit of keeping up with contacts:

- In which areas beyond high school are you interested in making new contacts?

- Who might you want more information or contact from to further your interests?

- What system have you set to check in on a timely basis to not miss messages and opportunities?

Closing Advice

I discovered a few more strategies when going through this with my own kids. In dealing with this topic, try to be more Socratic, asking questions versus telling your teen what they should do. Because they are developing independence, your teen may not always appreciate this line of conversation about an area of their life over which they believe they have control. Remember that an adult point of view can be helpful in considering how others in the web community will view, make assumptions, and use the information offered. Try to connect your teen to other adults your student values and/or perceives as having expertise in areas they'd like to pursue beyond high school. Finally, be careful with your own posts and comments on your social media channels. You might want to consider asking permission and giving your student veto power on things you share. Continuing to demonstrate mutual respect always goes a long way in building trust in your relationship.

Chapter 11
THE SENIOR SLUMP

How to identify and support your high schooler through senioritis

Casie Wise, EdD
High School English Teacher, Tennessee

In the past, I would have written this chapter solely from my career experience as a teacher. However, at the time of this writing, I am a parent of a senior who was recently deep in the trenches of the slump. In fact, my son's slump began the last semester of his junior year. The reality is that students can experience burnout at any point in their high school journey, even up to the incredible moment they officially graduate.

I am sure we all remember our own senior year but, as we search for the right words or motivating advice, we never quite remember the depth of our own challenges. We also must admit that our seniors' experiences may not be the same as ours because they are growing up in a different world than we did. But, thankfully, parents and caregivers are not alone in this. Teachers and school staff also want seniors to finish high school successfully.

I was a lead senior teacher for five years and saw firsthand how important it is to create spaces for students to challenge themselves and each other, while also providing opportunities for them to take breaks and build healthy habits as they make decisions about the future. I built relationships with the families of my students so that we could work together to keep students motivated. Even if seniors are accepted into college earlier in the year, their grades, activities, and community service matter up to the day they graduate. It is a collective effort to get them across that stage.

What is the Senior Slump?

We all have those moments when, no matter how hard you try, life seems to weigh you down. This can feel like a physical slouch, as your energy is drained and you cannot seem to pull yourself up. It can also be a slump in your emotional or mental health. Either way, a slump can be difficult to overcome. The Senior Slump is often called **senioritis**. Though it is certainly not a disease, it can still seem like something that is transmissible among peers, and it can plague students for long enough to become a problem. Simply put, senioritis is a decline in the motivation or initiative needed to finish an education journey successfully. While most students can be coached out of senioritis and many overcome it on their own, senioritis can harm a student's future possibilities. This is why the signs and recommendations in this chapter are important.

What Signs Should I Look for?

Senioritis can look different from one student to another, but there are some general warning signs that you should watch for. Keep in mind that senioritis can impact students at any time. Some students, like my son, experience the burnout or lack of motivation before even making it to senior year. Others may start 12th grade strong but lose steam midway through the year or even in the weeks leading up to graduation. The earlier the slump begins, the more detrimental it can be on grades and the college application process. Watch for the following signs:

- Low enthusiasm about school events, classes, or even friend groups
- Lack of concern about grades or academic performance
- Frequent requests to stay home from school (or skipping outright)
- Assumption that effort isn't necessary in the last year of school
- Minimal time spent on homework or projects
- Changes in mood or attitude that can affect relationships
- Excessive time spent sleeping or avoiding responsibilities

It does not necessarily indicate senioritis if your teen exhibits *one* of these behaviors. However, any one of these can lead to the others, so it is important to stay aware of what is going on in your teenager's life.

How Should I Respond if My Child has Senioritis?

There are definitive steps you can take to address senioritis. However, the first move is to determine *how* you will respond.

As parents preparing for our kids to graduate and most likely leave home, we can feel a heightened sense of urgency to prepare our seniors for the real world. When they do not respond with the same urgency, it can cause frustration and stress. The most important thing to remember about parenting through a senior year is to not add to the stress that your student may already feel. During a senior slump, your student may slack on responsibility or not respond the way you expect. Your instinct may be to hand out consequences or punishment, but it is more supportive if you show flexibility and patience while sharing perspective and understanding.

I can tell you from experience that this is exhausting. It is difficult to allow our kids the freedom to make certain choices or even mistakes. This does not mean that you should practice a hands-off approach; that would actually be detrimental to a senior. Instead, give your senior a chance to lead the decision-making process while you offer guidance. The following scenario is pulled directly from my engagement with my son early in the school year:

> Mom: How are classes going? Is calculus as hard as you thought it would be?
>
> Son: I decided not to take calculus.
>
> Mom (shocked): What?! When did this change? How?
>
> Son: I switched classes at the beginning of the year. I am taking statistics instead.
>
> Mom: But why would you do that? You chose to study physics in college, and you are going to need calculus for that. I don't understand how you can't see how important this is.
>
> Son: Mom, I know it is important. I just know how hard the teacher is. I barely made it through Advanced Math with her. Her classes are really hard.
>
> Mom: That does not make sense. Why would you do that rather than work hard and get the experience of calculus?
>
> Son: There is a real possibility that I could fail her class. Last year, most of the students in her calculus class got really bad grades. I do not want to hurt my GPA or fail. There is too much going on for that kind of stress.

Mom: Well, it sounds like you made a solid decision based on what you thought was best for you this year. Though I may not agree, I can understand why you made this choice, and this is an example of the choices you will need to make in college. What I am going to ask you to do is take an online calculus practice course. Or we can purchase a calculus workbook. I still feel that you need some practice before starting your physics program. Is that a deal?

Son: Yeah, that works for me. Thanks, Mom.

In this scenario, I made some assumptions about my son's choice and reacted too quickly up front. I learned that I need to give him time to process and explain his decisions. Though I felt like I had his best interests in mind, he presented a solid explanation as to why his choice to change classes was going to keep him from being overly stressed. I offered a solution that supported his decision but also ensured he could still engage with calculus concepts before taking the course in college. I had to realize the added stress of a very difficult class that he could fail was worse than not having the class completed prior to college.

What Can I Do to Support My Senior?

Though I will share a list of recommendations here, the one word that summarizes everything is **patience**. Yes, that seems to always be on the list of parenting tricks, but if ever there was a time to practice patience beyond your normal ability, it is during senior year. With a roller-coaster ride that peaks with excitement only to be followed by fear and uncertainty, believe that your senior, who may appear to be unbothered, is shaky inside. There are so many things that happen during senior year—many of which we do not even see, because we are not at school with our kids. A true demonstration of patience speaks volumes to your teenager and indicates that you see them and recognize their challenges.

After several heated debates with my son, I realized two things: We had accomplished very little and I was alienating him, and showing patience was not a weakness; instead, it gave my son time to build his own self-awareness and autonomy. I had to change the way that I was responding to him, which meant pausing and listening rather than immediately showing my frustration. I sought advice on how to better guide my son through the year from his school staff, other parents, and counselors. These are some of the things I have learned from my experience:

Set goals together

I am an educator who sets goals regularly in my work, but I had not done this intentionally with my son. We had plenty of talks about what college would be like and what he could see himself studying, but we did not write down or capture short- and long-term goals that he could use to measure his progress. Depending on how intensely your child is experiencing senioritis, goal setting could be a daily practice to give your child small wins each day. For my son, we set goals for the school year and summer leading up to college. Then, we worked backward, to create smaller goals under those that he could reach monthly or by certain dates. We put reminders in our phones for our progress check-ins. We made this more engaging by doing our check-in over dinner or at one of his favorite food spots. I realized that his being able to see his progress was motivating for him.

Encouraging your senior to set goals may sound like this:

- "You told me that you have an idea of what you want to study in college. Why don't we sit down together and look at some schools?"

- "This college application looks a bit time-consuming. Let's see how we can divide this up over a few days to get it done."
- "I heard you tell Grandma that you want to buy a really good laptop for school next year. Would you be open to setting some savings goals and thinking of ways to earn money?"
- "It sounds like your senior English class is causing some stress with the heavy writing load. Let's set some daily goals for this week to complete your essay assignment on time."

Provide attainable rewards or incentives

We can sometimes mistake the excitement and expenses of a senior year as rewards for student success. However, our kids still need us to recognize smaller wins, especially if they have set goals for self-care, academic performance, scholarship applications, community service, or maintaining the balance between school and a job. It can be helpful to boost initiative if we teach our children to set their own incentives and we match them. For example, because my son wants to attend an out-of-state school, he needed to work during his senior year and summer to save for future tuition. To help him see his time translate to money, we opened a high-yield savings account. To incentivize my son to save as much of his paycheck as he could, I offered to match the 5% interest that he made each month. I told him that once he reached a certain level in his bank account, I would double that to 10%. While monetary incentives may not always be possible, this example shows the importance of matching or rewarding your child's investment in something.

Be flexible and forgiving

This is advice for both you and your high schooler. Senior year is challenging territory, and we are bound to make mistakes. Often, students find that teachers are more patient with them because this is something that teachers experience with many students each year. Parents and seniors are going to feel the stress and anxiousness of this huge step into adulthood. You and your teen are going through this together. Giving each other grace and being open to give and ask for forgiveness is critical to fostering a healthy relationship. This is even more important as our seniors are becoming legal adults while struggling with what adulthood means emotionally, physically, economically, and socially. The best we can do is model how to be forgiving, admit mistakes, correct them, and move on. Here is an example that happened with my son:

Son: Hey Mom, I need to stay after school today.

Mom (with frustrated tone): Why?

Son: I need to retake my computer science test from last week. Ummm, I failed it.

Mom: How could you fail that? You like computers and that class should be easy for you. I guess I can't say no, because this is about your grade. But you need to do better. I'll have to shift my schedule to pick you up later.

Son: I'm sorry, Mom! Last week was really tough. I had three tests and an essay due. I had to pick what I thought was the most important thing to study for. At least Mr. Jones is letting me take it again.

Mom (breathes out): You're right. I recognize that you felt stressed about your work, and having to prioritize things is an important skill. I apologize for getting upset with you so easily. There is a lot going on in our lives. I'll make arrangements to pick you up later. How about the next time you have a rough week, let me know? I am here to help you, and it is okay to ask for help.

Model self-care

We hear more about mental health now than ever, especially after the COVID pandemic. Because of the increase in anxiety and mental health awareness, it is important to check in regularly with your teenager and model how to take care of yourself. Though we want our seniors to strive for excellence, we must also ensure that they do not sacrifice their well-being. We need to help them prioritize activities and let some things go. Encourage your senior to take breaks and time off, especially if you notice they are more anxious than normal. Show how to take breaks for yourself. Offer ways that your teen can rest and recharge on their own, as well as activities that you can do together, like taking walks in the park or classes at a recreation center, outdoor observations or relaxation, beauty or spa treatments, restaurant dining, museum visits, or creative projects.

Here are some other ways to encourage self-care:

- Practice intentional, positive mindsets. For example, when you and your senior leave or come home, practice leaving something stressful at the door and thinking of something positive to embrace.

- When something is difficult or stressful, call out how you feel and what is making you feel that way. Acknowledge that other people may feel that way, too, and that it is normal to experience this. Talk about how to practice kindness with yourself.

- Model activity that does not depend on technology. We all need time away from our tech, and our children need to see that we are willing to join them in this as well. Look for physical activities or relaxation techniques that engage the body and mind and give you time away from screens.

Affirm feelings and struggles as normal

This is advice from a parent who learned this lesson this past year. After a couple months of son vs. mom in our senior slump journey, my son finally shared that he was scared of failing his first semester of college, which is why he was acting nonchalant and trying to avoid applying for the college he wanted to attend. When I heard this, I was relieved and shocked at the same time. What I interpreted as being lazy was actually a deep-seated fear, and a fear that is very real for many seniors. My son could not see that being afraid to fail in college was completely normal. Going to college can be scary, and we need to acknowledge that these feelings are okay and can be overcome by addressing the fear and setting goals for success. Once we help our seniors acknowledge that fear, confusion, anger, and even avoidance are normal, we also should emphasize that we must move past these feelings, because they can eventually become barriers to success.

You might say:

- "It is completely natural for you to feel _____. That is what makes us human. What are some of the things about this year that make you feel this way?"
- "I hear you say that you are feeling _____. I remember feeling this way, too. It is normal, and I do not want you to be embarrassed about how you feel. Let's talk about some ways that we can work together to understand what is making you feel like this."

- "Can you tell me more about what you are feeling? It is completely normal, but I want you to get more comfortable sharing your feelings. This is a safe space, and I will listen openly."

Celebrate the wins, big and small

Senior year is a team effort. Your team includes community, extended family, school staff, friends, and anyone else who engages with your child. The old saying, "It takes a village to raise a child," is still true, and that entire village needs to celebrate that child, too, from things as small as maintaining their chores around the house, completing homework on time, or being a part of school events, to the major senior milestones of college acceptance, drivers' licenses, scholarships, and more. Celebrating even the small things boosts motivation for young people and lets them know that their family and community see them and support them.

Closing Advice

Six months ago, I could not have foreseen my son's college acceptance moment. I could not have imagined the conversations we would have, the jobs he would apply for, and the impact his senior year would have on our family. We have made our mistakes and learned from them together, and I would not trade this experience for anything. Whether you are about to enter the senior year journey with your child or are almost through it, I encourage you not to go through it alone. Build a support group. Establish close connections with teachers and community members. You have already started out on the right path by reading this book. I am cheering you on.

Chapter 12
FINDING WHAT YOU LOVE TO DO...IN AND OUT OF SCHOOL

How the search for passions extends past high school

Laura Jeanne Penrod
2024 Nevada State Teacher of the Year

From a young age, we are frequently asked, "What do you want to be when you grow up?" I have learned from this question that we are simply doing a disservice to our young people by asking them what they want to be. We need to start asking them, "*Who* do you want to be?" I say this simply because everything seems fun when we are young children. I thought being a veterinarian would be fun when I was five. At 15, when I came to the emotional realization that I could never save all the animals, I knew loving animals and having a profession working to keep them wasn't for me any longer. I am a proud pet owner today, and though I love my animal companions, my passion is not personally attempting to save them with my love.

Passion and love for something are two different things. Passion will push us despite the difficulty. We want love to be easy, with less effort, though we know it is not; we don't approach love with the same enthusiasm as our passions. We can love our dogs, cats, phones, nature, hiking, weight-lifting, and shopping, but they aren't always our passions and don't pay the bills most days. It can, but we rarely get both aligned perfectly. It is impossible without life experience, work experience, and the maturity of a fully developed brain to know *what* we want to pursue as our passion in life. Still, it is easy to explore interests, and we can do that with:

1. Vulnerability

2. Curiosity

3. Risk-Taking

Step One: Vulnerability

The first step to supporting high school seniors in discovering their passions is for adults to be vulnerable with them. And though we frequently hide our insecurities and mistakes, it is the first step in getting our students to feel connected. Once students feel free to engage with an adult willing to share their most challenging difficulties on the way to their passions, or the mistakes or insecurities they have had along the way, they see the human side of adults. It is no longer an adult who knows it all, but an adult who, like them, was scared, maybe made turns that took them off the path to find something better, or took a risk that led to the greatest passion of their lives. Seniors LOVE stories, and they love them when they are at our expense. It allows them to not be the focus of everyone's attention. We all remember being in high school and wishing everyone would just leave us alone rather than asking us what we wanted to do with our lives or what we loved.

Create an environment of trust. Building trust with your young adult can be done in a variety of ways, but my favorite one is to allow them to ask you questions about life. Talking Point cards, the Teens pack, is a great resource that creates an open format for questions about anything and everything. It takes the focus off academics and moves to generalized questions, creating a bridge between parent and teen. You can also talk about when you were a teen and how you would have answered the question. It might shock your teen into realizing the decisions you made as a teen would be different than what you would do today. By providing set questions, the conversation flows easily, and questions can be pulled randomly by you or your teen to provide a true sense of connection without forcing it.

Another way to create vulnerability is to invite your teen to ask questions about what it was like when you were in high school or college. Here are some sample questions:

- What did you initially have a passion for in high school or college? What made you not pursue that passion into adulthood?
- How did you choose/commit to the job/profession you are in now? Do you love it or tolerate it? If you love it, how did you know it was your passion? If you tolerate it, what is your passion, and why don't you pursue it?
- What are some of the passions you have in your career/job? What are passions you have outside of work?
- When you went to college, what was the most common major? Why did you or didn't you pursue it?
- What is a regret you have? Do you wish you had found a passion sooner in life?
- How do you handle setbacks when pursuing your passions?
- What has been the most challenging obstacle in pursuing your passions?

- What experiences (i.e., travel, school, roommates, jobs, hobbies, internships, fellowships) have helped you learn more about your passions?
- What words of advice would you give your 18- to 24-year-old self? Why?
- What passion do you currently want to pursue, and what are you doing to pursue it?
- What was your greatest fear as a graduating senior in high school? Why?
- How did you overcome your greatest fear as a young adult?
- What is your current fear, and what are you doing to work on it?
- What has helped you grow the most in your personal and professional life?
- Do you believe that forming quality relationships and networks is what helps you find your passions? Why or why not?
- What risk do you wish you had taken as a senior in high school?

This list of questions can help you start to be vulnerable with your young adult. When teens are allowed to see our journeys into our passions, careers, and interests, it lets them know that we, too, have had fears, goals, and desires. Some have worked out and some haven't. It is about failing forward and continuing to pursue our passions, regardless of age. We are all capable of growth, and the sooner our young adults see that development and the pursuit of our passions don't stop at a given age, the sooner they realize that the pursuit of those passions continues well beyond senior year of high school.

Step Two: Curiosity

Past elementary school, students need more opportunities to explore their interests in school. Yes, electives are an option, but, frequently, they are chosen at the middle and high school levels because friends are joining them, they fulfill college requirements, they look good on a résumé, or, worse, because your student ran out of options and chose something they didn't want to.

Adam Grant, the author of *Think Again: The Power of Knowing What You Don't Know*, states that to live whole lives, we must remain curious and treat life like scientists, constantly questioning and exploring our knowledge and understanding of life. Essentially, we must play purposefully to find our passions. But how do we do this, and how do we help our young adults do this? We teach them to ask beautiful questions about their lives to help them find their passions.

What are beautiful questions? According to Warren Berger and Elise Foster in their book, *Beautiful Questions for the Classroom*, a beautiful question can be considered **presence + vulnerability + making an actual invitation**, one that allows for an honest, open-ended conversation to happen with wonderment. There are many ways to approach beautiful questions. Still, it starts with being present, setting up the vulnerability, and inviting your young adult to feel comfortable asking questions. Questions allow teens to explore who they are and who they want to be, not *what* they want to be. Examples of beautiful questions with teens:

- Why do we do what we do as humans? How can we learn what we do and don't want to explore or pursue as passions?
- What is someone's passion you admire, and why do you feel attracted to that passion (i.e., ease, money, enjoyment)?
- How do you feel about the concept of time? Will this shift for you as you age?
- In the spirit of fresh beginnings, if your life were a book, what would the current chapter be titled, and what might be its opening lines?

- In the spirit of the future, if you were to title your book, what would be the title, the name of the first chapter, and the opening lines?
- As a senior in high school, what are the top three things you would tell your 8th-grade self?
- If you could know everything that will happen in your life, would you want to live it exactly as it plays out or try to control your destiny?
- If you could plant a seed in your garden of possibility and wonder, what dream are you nurturing to become a reality? What extraordinary accomplishments do you want to be part of your vision?
- If money were no object, what passion would you pursue?
- Grades are not the only determiner of success in life. What do you enjoy doing but didn't excel at in school? Could you enjoy this if there was no grade attached to it?
- Out of all the life experiences you have had thus far, what are the top three experiences you could see yourself pursuing as a passion in adult life? What would stop you from pursuing these?
- Beyond school or work titles, what's a role or identity you carry with pride? How has that shaped your journey so far?

Beautiful questions invite the conversation into a space of exploration in the *what-if* without committing to a correct answer. High school seniors often have a deep-rooted fear of making mistakes and picking the wrong major, wasting time, and starting over again. We need to teach our young adult learners that there is no wasted time, but options explored. They will learn what they do and do not like much faster by having the freedom to choose what is and is not a fit. If we support this style of dreaming and exploration, the question moves from what I want to be to how I want to show up in my passions and interests. Of course, we don't want to waste money, time, effort, etc., but sometimes those things must occur to get to the other side of learning and exploring our passions. Allowing our teens to be less definite in their responses to beautiful questions and more curious opens up a window of opportunity to play or explore who they want to be.

Step Three: Risk-Taking

The last step in supporting our young adult learners in their passions is encouraging risk-taking. When I was a senior in high school, my beloved psychology teacher taught me that the only free people in the world are those who risk everything to follow their dreams, passions, and desires. That statement was out of my comfort zone at the time, but that is because I didn't have a support system that fostered failing anywhere in life as an option. There was only a soft place to land if I succeeded. If no one was there to support me, I wasn't willing to take action. As an adult with a lot of life experience, I recognize that the best opportunities have come my way out of sheer risk-taking and starting well before I thought I was ready to pursue whatever dreams those were. I would have done so sooner if I had had a soft place to land.

As a student support system, we must foster a sense of security in failing forward. If our young adult learners want to find their passions, they must feel safe to fail. They have to know that they won't be held to the fire for not pursuing a passion they initially thought they would love. It is our responsibility to foster a sense of risk-taking with growth. The best gift we can give them is the opportunity to try to be successful, not be successful to try. Implementing a solid sense of safety in risk-taking will allow their passions to blossom and eventually become something more beautiful than we could've imagined.

Closing Advice

There is no one *right* way to foster passion for young adult learners to take with them as they finish high school. We need to let them explore with safety, ask beautiful questions that allow them to wonder and dream without timelines and requirements, and enable them to see that we are not ever where we fully want to be in life as an adult. We are *all* still growing. Teach them that there is no correct answer, only the answer that will help lead them to the next destination they dream up. The journey is part of finding your passions—it is not how we got there, but that we did.

Chapter 13
CONGRATULATIONS, YOU HAVE A SENIOR!

How will I know if my teen is ready for what's next?

Jessica Volker
South Dakota State Teacher of the Year Finalist

Senior year. The culmination of not only high school, but also *years* of school. You, as the parent of a soon-to-be or new senior, may feel all sorts of emotions like excitement, eagerness, dread, and anxiety. As much as you are experiencing these emotions, they most likely are in your soon-to-be adult as well. They just may not know how to identify and articulate those feelings. Seniors face enormous pressure as they experience the "lasts" of their K–12 education. Bombarded with the question, "What are your plans for next year?", they are hit from every side with expectations, assumptions, and the unknown. Emotionally, this can be exciting and taxing. While your student may have excitement and energy for what lies ahead, it is also possible that doubts about their post-high school decision may begin to creep in, because they will be leaving what they have always known behind. Your teen may be feeling a lot of pressure about the decisions for "what's next."

I have taught high school seniors for the last 13 years and have seen seniors go in many different directions after high school. I have been asked numerous questions by students and parents about what's next after high school graduation. This chapter is organized around those questions, along with practical tips, conversation starters, and ideas for you to help your senior throughout the school year.

How Do I Know How My Senior is Feeling About What is Next if They Won't Talk About It?

Don't be alarmed if your senior doesn't know how to voice their feelings throughout the year, and certainly don't be alarmed if those feelings change quite often. Some seniors lean into all of the *lasts* (i.e., last high school game or concert, last homecoming, last prom, last year with all of their peers) and soak these up in every way possible. Maybe your senior has already taken enough credits to graduate, so they are filling their schedule with electives. Maybe your senior is taking Advanced Placement (AP) classes and is stressed about preparing for AP tests in the spring. Depending on where your senior falls, they may start to get bored at school or not see the purpose. Your senior may have a large case of "senioritis" and suddenly procrastinate when they never have before. Simply put, if their behavior is different from previous years, it's probably because they are looking ahead to what is to come, while also trying to figure out how to stay present and enjoy the year. What a combination of emotions!

Here are some great conversation starters to use to check in with your child, both early on (during the summer before senior year begins) and during the school year:

- How do you feel about what comes after high school graduation? Do you know what is making you feel this way?
- Are there any job fairs you'd like to attend?
- Are there any colleges you'd like to visit?
- Are there any nonprofit organizations where you can volunteer?
- Are there any businesses you'd like to contact regarding a position next year?

What Are the Post-Graduation Options for My Senior?

The traditional route of a senior attending college following graduation may not appeal to your child. Good news: There are lots of options for postsecondary life. It is important to know that what you experienced growing up may not even be close to the journey that your child is going to take. And that is okay. Take the pressure off yourself and your child in case a four-year degree isn't really what they want to do. Ask your child about their interests and what they imagine doing in the future, and continue to have those conversations as the year unfolds. The most important thing you can do is find out what *they* want to do, and let your student dream. And don't freak out when one day they say they want to travel the world after graduation instead of going to school—that idea could very well change next month when their friends are all applying for housing at their colleges. Below are some common options that are available for seniors after high school graduation:

- **Four-year college or university:** This route is what previous generations may have taken and what many seniors feel like is the expected next step. It is still a common avenue, but sometimes it is pursued for the wrong reasons. Kids today are more aware of student loan debt and finances than any generation before, so your child may be thinking of a different way into a job without having to pay for this much school. On the flip side, many students have a path that requires a four-year degree (i.e., majors in nursing, computer science, engineering, and business). Look into scholarships, programs of study at schools, and job opportunities specifically related to your teen's major to help guide this decision. Check college entrance requirements to know what your student needs (more on this below).

- **Two-year trade school (also called vocational or technical school):** This option is for students who want to specialize in technical skills and abilities. These students don't take the general education courses that a four-year degree requires; they stick to classes that teach the skills needed for their chosen field. They might be training to become an electrician, plumber, automotive mechanic, or welder, for example.
- **Community college:** A community college is typically a two-year school that students attend based on their affordability and options for degrees. Community colleges offer a wide variety of associates degrees and credits are generally transferable to four-year schools if your student wants to continue after two years. Associates degrees are pursued for a variety of reasons, but they can also be used as a pathway to a Bachelor's Degree at a four-year school. Many community colleges are continuing to expand their facilities for students to even include student clubs/organizations and housing facilities. Students can earn an Associate of Arts or Associate of Science degree, which are necessary for many jobs such as radiologic technologist, respiratory therapist, web developer, and many more. See the vocational/technical school section above for a more specific type of community college.

- **Gap year or work:** A gap year is when a senior wants to take at least one year of nonacademic study before deciding which direction to go in the future. This can look different for every student. Some students take a gap year to work for a nonprofit organization (see Service Year Alliance [serviceyear.org] for many potential opportunities) or travel. Others want to join the workforce right away because they want to save money before looking into higher education.
- **Military:** Perhaps members of your family served in the military. Maybe your student met with a recruiter during their freshman or sophomore year when the National Guard visited their school, and they are already helping them in town. Sometimes students consider mixing enlistment and school at the same time by applying to a school like The United States Military Academy at West Point.
- **Family business:** Whether managing gas stations or running the machines at your family farm, a family business is an option some kids like to take. It is what they are passionate about, what they see themselves doing long-term, and, most likely, what they have observed you doing throughout their life.

How Do I Know if My Student is Academically Prepared for Next Year?

For a four-year, two-year, or military school, graduating high school is required. Check in with your senior and their counselor to ensure that they have taken all of the required courses and have enough credits to graduate. Many jobs today also require a high school diploma, so if your senior is planning to go into the workforce immediately, check that they that they have met all their requirements and are all set to graduate.

Four-year school

Your student should take the ACT and/or SAT (depending on what college they want to attend). Some states require students to take the ACT their junior year, while other states do not. Check to make sure that your senior has taken the appropriate test and has a few opportunities to take it again if they aren't satisfied with their score. If your senior has room in their schedule and has taken the prerequisites, have them sign up for college and/or Advanced Placement (AP) classes their senior year. College credit typically tends to be cheaper when the class is taken in high school, and sometimes students can take so many classes that they are already a semester or two ahead in college. Your senior should maintain their grade point average or even work to keep improving it, because some colleges require a high GPA.

Two-year trade school

If your senior has room in their schedule and your high school offers career and technical education (CTE) classes, they should sign up for those that seem interesting to see if it is something they actually want to do. Examples of CTE classes that some high schools offer include welding, automotive repair, robotics, and video production. Encourage your senior to continue to maintain a strong GPA as they apply to schools.

Community college

Different community colleges may have different requirements. Be sure to look at specific ones your student is interested in. Community colleges will require a high school diploma or GED. Depending on the type of program that your student is pursuing, some community colleges may require an ACT or SAT score. Community colleges are similar to technical and vocational schools.

Gap year/workforce

Financial topics like creating a budget and understanding insurance are important for the senior who is entering the workforce or taking a gap year. A course that is useful for all seniors—and typically a high school graduation requirement—is personal finance, which will be especially beneficial for your senior if they are going to step out immediately on their own.

Military

A high school diploma is required for entering the military. Depending on which branch of the armed forces your senior wants to enlist in, there is a placement test that they will need to pass. While this is not the ACT or SAT, the basic knowledge and skills that they learned in high school will be crucial for this test. Don't hesitate to ask a recruiter for more information. If you are unsure of how to contact a recruiter, a high school counselor will have contact information.

How Do I Know if My Child is Emotionally Prepared for Next Year?

Depending on what route they take, your child may be hit with a ton of independent responsibilities or may be undertaking more of a gradual role into adulthood. While we hope that high school prepares them for the "real world," there could be some things that they either (a) don't remember or (b) don't know. How do they handle stress? How are they with time management? Do you still have to wake them up to get to school on time? Do they feel confident in providing for themselves (like changing a car tire) and advocating when they need something (like a missing assignment)? These questions are a great place to start when thinking about helping them grow into their independence.

How Do I Know if My Child Has Taken Care of the Senior Year Checklist?

The checklist depends on what option your student is planning on taking. The list below covers a variety of topics and tasks for your senior to complete by the end of high school.

Senior Year Checklist

August/September

- ☐ Double-check with the high school counselor that all required classes have been taken (or are signed up for) to fulfill graduation requirements.
- ☐ Sign up for the ACT that is offered in September, October, December, February, and April (locations and availability change per month).
- ☐ Sign up for the SAT if the college you have chosen requires it. Typically this test is offered four times a year, so check in with the high school counselor to see the dates and times.
- ☐ Set up any final college visits.
- ☐ Apply for any colleges as soon as possible (each college has a different deadline, but typically applications should be in by October 31; use the Common App if possible, as it keeps your information together in one place).
- ☐ Schedule a meeting with your counselor to create a calendar that shows when scholarships for the colleges you are applying to become available and their deadlines.
- ☐ Meet with a recruiter early in the year if you are enlisting.

October/November

- ☐ Ensure your college applications have been submitted or, if they have a later deadline, continue working on them.
- ☐ Complete the FAFSA and any other financial aid forms.
- ☐ Begin applying for scholarships. Some scholarships require an essay (see the Common App), and many require letters of recommendation from teachers. Begin working on the essay and reaching out to teachers now to ensure that they are ready for the deadline.
- ☐ If you are looking into a gap year and working for a nonprofit, begin researching options. Some of these programs start in January or begin selecting individuals in early spring.

December/January

- ☐ Continue working on scholarship applications. Send reminders to teachers for their letters of recommendation. Have someone help edit your essay.
- ☐ If you still need to apply for a school, contact the admissions office (there may be a late fee at this point).
- ☐ Double-check that all of your applications have been submitted to the correct place.
- ☐ Order your cap and gown through the school. Typically, there is a senior class meeting with this information.

February/March

- ☐ Begin completing requirements for college housing/registration/etc. for next year.
- ☐ Work with parent to send out graduation invites to family and friends (if desired).

- [ ] Work with parent to plan a graduation celebration for May/June (if desired).

May/June

- [ ] Get final transcripts from your high school. These typically are not ready before the graduation ceremony, and you may have to stop by the school a week or so after.
- [ ] Continue working on required documents needed for the path you are taking after graduation.
- [ ] Celebrate this milestone with your family!

www.ingramcontent.com/pod-product-compliance
Lightning Source LLC
Chambersburg PA
CBHW011758040426
42446CB00018B/3453